The Wasted Land

by Gerald W. Johnson

A WASTED LAND, but a land so rich that it is not yet too late to make it the garden of the world; a wasted people, but a people so full of potential energy as to be able to perfect a social order fruitful in and for the lives of men; a Southern region "capable of growing every crop that can be grown anywhere in the United States," but given over to a collapsing one-crop system—this is what Gerald Johnson sees when he looks below the Potomac.

His warning is sharp; his challenge, stern. There appears to be no middle ground for the Southeast, he says, "between a high civilization and something indistinguishable from semi-barbarism," between "the horror portrayed in *Tobacco Road*" and an agriculture developed far beyond that of other sections. The complete wreck of the cotton economy is plainly in sight; and with a waste "so titanic as to be incomprehensible"—97,000,000 acres of land made useless by erosion, leaching, and over-cropping, and 3,500,000 men lost by emigration alone—"fifty years more of waste at the present rate will do the work which, once done, cannot be undone save by the work of centuries, if at all."

This state of things, however, he believes to be "avoidable and remediable" by the Southern people themselves. That they can rescue the South from its suicidal waste, he has no doubt; that they will do so, he is not so certain, for the problem is regional, and the solution is regional, and people must learn to think and plan regionally, rather than in terms of the separate States.

The Wasted Land

THE
WASTED LAND

GERALD W. JOHNSON

The University of North Carolina Press
CHAPEL HILL
1937

THE UNIVERSITY OF NORTH CAROLINA PRESS, CHAPEL HILL, N. C.; THE BAKER AND TAYLOR COMPANY, NEW YORK; OXFORD UNIVERSITY PRESS, LONDON; MARUZEN-KABUSHIKI-KAISHA, TOKYO; EDWARD EVANS & SONS, LTD., SHANGHAI; D. B. CENTEN'S WETENSCHAPPELIJKE BOEKHANDEL, AMSTERDAM.

Foreword

TO MANY AMERICANS THE SOCIAL HISTORY OF the United States between 1926 and 1936 reads like a chapter out of the annals of some strange and unheard-of land. Factors in our economic and social life which we had believed to be as immutable as the eternal hills have developed a trick of evaporating almost between sun and sun; and appearances which we had taken for mist and mirage have as suddenly displayed the solidity and massiveness of the Appalachian chain. This is certainly not the America of 1926, nor does it seem probable that we shall ever see that country again.

Nowhere have the changes been swifter or more radical than in the southern part of the republic. Efforts have recently been made to determine with some precision the position of the South in this new country; nor have these efforts come any too soon. In the pages that follow some of the findings recently made are sketched—not presented, merely sketched—first, for the information of readers whose time does not permit them to examine the scientific reports, and then for the convenience of students who desire an introduction to serious study of the subject.

This book is essentially a commentary on *Southern Regions of the United States,* written by Howard W. Odum for the Southern Regional Committee of the Social Science Research Council, under whose auspices the Southern Regional Study was undertaken. But this is a commentary, not merely a *précis;* that is to say, while nearly all the facts are taken from *Southern Regions,* many of the inferences drawn from the facts are my own, and it is necessary to absolve Dr. Odum and his colleagues from responsibility for opinions they did not express and with which they are not necessarily in agreement.

CONTENTS

The Wasted Land

1. *Question and Challenge*

CAN THE SOUTH, GIVEN TIME AND IMMUNITY from earthquake, pestilence and invasion by armed enemies, regain a position relatively as important in the Union as the one it held between 1776 and 1860?

The impulse of the patriotic Southerner is to answer, "Yes, of course," but this answer is, in part, erroneous. The error is in the emphasis. The "yes" is right, but the "of course" is all wrong. It is better to say, the South *may* regain its position; it is safer yet to say, the South *might* regain its position; but to assert flatly that the South *will* do so, supposing it escapes calamity from without, is to take a much stronger line than the facts warrant.

Granting that the region has exhibited splendid energy and vitality, especially since the turn of the century, the fact remains that there are even now tremendous forces of destruction at work in the South. Recently there has been increasing reason to believe that these forces are gaining on the forces of construction, and it is by no means unimaginable that they may eventually become dominant, sweeping the region back to a level of civilization far lower than that which it occupies today. The destiny of the

South is not yet fixed and determined. Apparently its opportunity is great; but to improve that opportunity will require great wisdom, great tenacity and great labor. The existence of the opportunity is demonstrable by examination of objective fact; but the existence of the necessary wisdom, tenacity and industry is not demonstrable at all. On the contrary, it is evident without demonstration that they have not existed in the past in the measure required, for, if they had, the South would already occupy a position very much higher than the position it does occupy.

All the history of the world confirms the belief that the production of a great civilization is enormously facilitated by three natural advantages, to wit, fertile soil, a long growing season, and abundant rainfall. In all of these the southeastern part of the United States is often reputed to be better favored than any other region of comparable size, save one, anywhere on the globe. In addition to these it possesses enormous natural wealth in quarries, mines, oil fields, forests and fisheries. It has a long coast line with an adequate number of good harbors; its rivers supply many thousands of miles of available waterways; its railway system compares favorably with that of the rest of the country, and its highway system is in some respects better than the average for the country as a whole.

Favorable climate, fertility, mineral wealth, easy transportation and man-power are everywhere admitted to be the bases of national wealth. Yet, although it is in an advantageous position with regard to every one of these, the South remains the poorest of the regions into which the country is naturally divided. This anomaly can be explained in one word—waste. It cannot be explained in any other way.

Naturally Southerners have found other explanations more flattering to their self-esteem, but none of these other explanations stands up under critical examination. The two that are most commonly advanced are the problems presented by a bi-racial population, and the destruction that accompanied and followed a disastrous war. There is a measure of truth in both these explanations. The problems that they involve are certainly no figments of the imagination, but they do not account for the present low estate of the region. The presence of the Negro complicates every social, political and economic phase of Southern life; but his presence likewise adds millions of brawny laborers to the South's available man-power. Intelligently handled, it is very efficient labor, too; but it is, to say the least, open to doubt that the South has ever handled the Negro in such a way as to make him the most valuable asset he is capable of becoming.

As for the war, firing ceased more than seventy years ago. Two full generations have lived since the end of the conflict. If the South has not recovered from the war by this time, then it is idle to expect it ever to recover. Indeed, it is easy enough to see, now, that the economy under which the South was operating before 1860 was virtually in a state of collapse when the war struck it; had there been no war, slave labor and a one-crop agricultural system would have proved ruinous, just the same.

It is arguable that the most serious injury inflicted on the South by the war of the sixties was not the material and moral destruction that it caused, not the bloodshed, not the aftermath of Reconstruction, but simply the providing of a convenient scapegoat on which the South could lay the blame for all its subsequent economic, social and political failures. Had our economy crashed without a war, then we might have searched more diligently and more intelligently for the economic causes of that collapse, instead of attributing everything unpleasant to the military calamity.

By the same reasoning, the most encouraging factor in the life of the modern South, the thing that makes it possible to believe in her capacity to regain her old estate, to produce new Washingtons, Marshalls, Jeffersons, Madisons, new Declarations of Independence, new Constitutions, new theories of jurisprudence, of statecraft, new ornaments and monuments of civilization, is precisely her new disposition to probe ruthlessly for the truth about herself. There is still far too much blind allegiance to decrepit tradition, too much bland obliviousness of fact, too much complacent and willful ignorance, to be sure; but there is also among the more alert intelligences in the region a growing determination to know the truth in the belief that the truth will make us free.

Most notable among efforts along this line is the monumental inventory recently completed for the Southern Regional Committee by Howard W. Odum, in *Southern Regions of the United States*. This huge volume lays bare with the precision attainable only by the statistical method the exact condition of the South, not as it has been, not as it may be, but as it is now. Potentialities are not omitted, and the more obvious lines to be followed in the immediate future are indicated; but these, after all, are as much elements of the existing situation as are the cotton mills now in operation and the farms now tilled by tenant croppers. Historical perspective is essential to any adequate understanding of the South, of course; and a vision of its possible future must arise from any adequate understanding; but the great need of Southerners who wish to be useful to their native land is a larger comprehension of the South as it exists at this moment.

The first and deepest impression made upon one who examines the facts is the impression of waste so titanic as to be incomprehensible. It invades every department of life. It includes wasted men, wasted money, wasted land, wasted time, wasted opportunity. Within the last thirty years the South has thrown away three and a half million people. This represents the difference between emigration and immigration in that period; these are the Southerners who have been denied opportunity in their native region and therefore have sought it elsewhere, their contribution to civilization being lost to the South.

The South has thrown away ninety-seven million acres of land. This is an area larger than the two Carolinas and Georgia combined. It has been thrown away by the process of erosion, which has heavily damaged all of it and ren-

7

dered perhaps thirty million acres—almost as much as the whole State of North Carolina—unfit for any use.

The South has wasted time certainly to the extent of eighty years, for its losses by emigration, erosion and the one-crop system were pointed out both loudly and clearly as early as 1857, when Helper denounced them in *The Impending Crisis*. Unfortunately, the exposition was made much too loudly, for the man's strident vehemence produced far more heat than light.

Yet to make the sweeping assertion that the South has wasted everything would be not merely unjust but obviously preposterous. After all, here are twenty-five million people, one-fifth of the population of the whole country, producing annually the second most valuable money crop in the United States, producing enormous quantities of manufactured goods, producing most of the country's oil, and a tremendous share of its food, producing children in such hordes as are seen nowhere else in the land, and, especially for the last decade or so, producing books, plays and even symphony orchestras.

The South may be a spendthrift, but it is no idle waster. On the contrary, there is something emotionally moving in the magnitude of its labors; if its success in solving its problems has been but indifferent, it is not for lack of energy and courage in attacking them. They are, indeed, gigantic problems, and again and again the South has made gigantic efforts in grappling with them. The problem of public education, for example, has not been solved. It is further from solution in the South than in any other region. But when one considers that the South has to teach more Negro children than there are children of all kinds in New England; and when one notes that it is spending far more of its total income on schools than is spent by any other region, its effort, even though but half successful, must command respect and admiration.

There is no little pathos in the spectacle of the modern South. Confronted with immense and immensely complicated problems, it has frequently evinced a gallantry, a devotion and a spirit of self-sacrifice that deserve a success far greater than any it has achieved. But if there is something pathetic, there is also something irritating in the spectacle of tremendous efforts being made largely without intelligent direction, the spectacle of a strong and energetic people thrashing around blindly rather than pursuing a reasonably logical and intelligent course.

It is incontestably true that a stupid economy and a blind social polity are characteristically human, rather than characteristically Southern. The candid observer set down in any country in any part of the world today will see around him plenty of evidence that the Southern States have no monopoly of bad economics and worse statecraft. The best that human wisdom has been able to provide falls far short of meeting the need. But when a region is conspicuously rich and the people who inhabit it are conspicuously poor, it is a fair presumption that their economy and statecraft are not up to the average, poor as that is by comparison with the ideal.

By comparison with the rest of the United States the

9

South is very rich and Southerners are very poor. This is the inescapable conclusion drawn from the facts presented in *Southern Regions*. Nor is the low estate of Southerners confined to poverty of the purse, compensated by an exceptional richness of culture. The South has, it is true, certain cultural assets potentially of enormous value. Its history, for example, is long. It comprises the oldest English-speaking communities in the Western hemisphere. Its folklore is prodigious, both in quantity and in color, variety and drama. Its recorded history is singularly colorful and romantic and contains countless pages splendid enough to build up a monumental nationalistic pride. It has the tradition of a social code of extraordinary grace and charm.

But this cultural treasure, like its physical riches, has been exploited with but indifferent success. Southern literature has, indeed, burst into a sudden flowering within the last decade, which, if continued, may soon bring the region into a favorable relation with any other section of the country; but the music which the world regards as distinctively Southern was, for the most part, produced either by Stephen Foster, a Pennsylvanian, or by some anonymous Negro troubadour, neither of whom drew upon the cultural resources of the region for his inspiration; the Southern theater shows some signs of life, but it certainly isn't dominant in the country; Southern painting and sculpture are almost non-existent; Southern architecture has produced nothing both original and indisputably of the first rank since Robert Mills, of Charleston, designed the Washington monument in 1848; and Southern scholarship is represented most largely and most brilliantly by the hordes of Southern-born professors who crowd Northern universities.

Whether one assays its physical wealth or its spiritual wealth the result is the same—the South has much and uses little; or rather, it displays relatively small intelligence in the use it makes of them, and therefore derives a relatively small return from its immense possessions.

There are, according to Odum, five major bases of a great civilization, two primary and three secondary. The two primary bases, natural wealth and human wealth, the South has in abundance; but she fails to derive full profit from them because she is deficient in the three secondary bases, to wit, technological skill, artificial wealth—money, capital, credit, or whatever you choose to call it—and institutional services.

The thing that makes a regional study of this sort worth while is the fact that Southern deficiencies are all in those things which may be supplied by intelligent effort. Human ingenuity has never yet solved the problem of supplying abundant rainfall to a dry country; but the problem of supplying technological skill where it is needed presents no insuperable difficulty to an energetic people. Artificial wealth, by its very definition, is created by intelligent effort, and institutional services can be maintained by it.

If the problem, then, is not a problem of erecting a whole new civilization, but of supplying deficiencies in a civilization already existing and possessing great strength in certain of its elements, it is obviously a prime necessity to know precisely what and where the deficiencies are, and, as near as may be, their exact size. Moreover, since the available energy and resources of the South are limited, it is important to know which deficiencies demand first attention and which may safely be held over for later treatment. These considerations, plus the element of timeliness, lend importance to the regional survey.

That element of timeliness deserves special emphasis. Perhaps it requires, too, some explanation, since it is not immediately apparent to every Southerner. The Southern States have recently astonished the nation with a tremendous display of energy. During the first quarter of the century the strides made along certain lines of development were prodigious. Industrialization, for example, proceeded further in that time than it had in any previous period four times as long. Public education moved almost as rapidly, and social services of all kinds made appearances in sections that had never known them before. The creation of artificial wealth proceeded apace. Gigantic individual fortunes were amassed in the South for the first time, and, what is more important, large numbers of Southerners acquired enough money to begin to think of themselves consciously as capitalists.

Most Southerners, looking upon these developments, have found them good. A few of the more far-sighted, or, perhaps, merely more pessimistic, seeing appear in the South the evils traditionally associated with industrialism, have questioned the value of the "progress" of the last generation. But rare indeed is the Southerner, whether enthusiastic supporter or critic of the New South, who has questioned the permanence of the advances made since the turn of the century.

Southern Regions, however, reveals the disturbing fact that there is a question, a serious question. The evidences of a failing civilization are sufficiently well known. Some of them are an increasing dispossession of the tillers of the soil or their reduction to a state bordering on peonage; increasing concentration of wealth in the hands of a progressively smaller group; a sort of mental and spiritual fatigue resulting in chauvinism and suspicion of new ideas; fanatical religious and social orthodoxy that resents fiercely any suggestion of a reëxamination of established concepts; the exacerbation of racial, sectarian and factional animosities; a growing distrust of the processes of government, reflected in an impatient refusal to tolerate the delays inseparable from the orderly administration of justice. All these are present in the South; and their presence certainly raises a question as to the permanence of its present level of civilization—nay, a question as to whether it has not already begun to subside.

Apart from these factors, however, economists already foresee plainly one tremendous crisis through which the South is bound to pass within a few years. The great money crop of the region, the crop on which its economy is based, is cotton; and it is clear that something definitely unpleasant is going to happen to cotton. The position of this fiber in world trade is being attacked from several directions. In the first place, the Southern United States no

longer possesses anything remotely approaching a monopoly of its production. Egypt, the Sudan, Brazil, India,
China, and even Russian Turkestan are all competitors
whose strength seems more likely to increase than to
diminish. In the second place, there are already in production several artificial fibers superior to cotton in certain
respects and very much cheaper. Every woman knows of
new fabrics that are more beautiful and cheaper than cotton. These artificial fibers have been steadily improving in
excellence and there is little reason to doubt that they will
be made better yet; which means that the market for cotton
is more likely to shrink than to expand in the near future.
Finally, there is every reason to believe that the mechanical
cotton-picker will be perfected soon, if, indeed, the thing
has not already been done. The effect of this will be to
stimulate cotton production in regions where it has been
handicapped by scarcity of labor for picking, specifically in
Texas, Oklahoma and Arizona, and to render superfluous
a large part of the farm population in the eastern part of
the region.

Altogether, it is hardly open to doubt that the South
cannot much longer rely on cotton as the foundation on
which to build a strong and enduring civilization. This
takes no account of the wave of intense nationalism sweeping over the world, which seems to threaten all international exchange of products. As cotton is an export crop,
nationalism, of course, damages it heavily; but if free trade
were established over the whole world tomorrow, cotton
would still be a precarious reliance, especially for the

Southeastern States. It is difficult to escape the conclusion that the existing economy of the South is soon to be forced into a reorganization that will subject it to some appalling stresses and strains.

For this reason, if for no other, the time element would be an extremely important factor in the equation. Every day that erosion is permitted to proceed unchecked, the South loses heavily. Every year that the one-crop system is permitted to rule, the restoration of the fertility of the soil becomes more difficult. Yet, swiftly as these menaces are approaching, they are by comparison slow processes. The dethronement of King Cotton is already an accomplished fact. Some unforeseen event—for instance, another war—might postpone the inevitable consequences for a few years, but the thing is done. In the absence of any extraordinary occurrence, it is idle to hope that cotton-growing will ever be a highly profitable enterprise again in the Southeastern States; and the probabilities favor a steadily declining price. This does not mean, of course, that there will not be years when for some special reason, such as a crop failure in the Southwest, the cotton crop of the South Atlantic and Gulf States will command a reasonably good price. Governmental action, comparable to the Agricultural Adjustment Administration, may force the price up for a time. A dozen factors may operate, and occasionally will operate, to enable the cotton farmer to sell his crop in some years at a price above the cost of production; but it is unlikely that the South can ever again look to this crop as a source of abundant and permanent prosperity.

15

The position of tobacco as a money crop is threatened, too, although not as seriously. The troubles of the Lady Nicotine are largely political. She is not facing rivals, as King Cotton is, in the form of satisfactory substitutes, nor is there any huge growing area likely to be developed in the near future. But tobacco is not only a luxury, but in half the world a government monopoly, therefore peculiarly subject to the whims and exigencies of politicians. The extreme nationalism of the modern world is the chief menace to tobacco; for this nationalism connotes a fierce objection to purchasing anything abroad. Efforts, frank, vigorous, and, from the American point of view, all too successful, are being made to restrict the purchase of American tobacco. Hence the only market to be relied on is the domestic market, which the tobacco fields of the South are capable of oversupplying in normal years.

The South has always been an agrarian region and seems likely to remain so indefinitely. It has developed a powerful industrialism within the last fifty years, and should develop it somewhat further; but there is no reason why it should, if it could, turn to industrialism as New England has. Yet if it is to remain primarily agrarian, and if the main support of its agricultural economy, cotton, is crumbling, while the secondary support, tobacco, is being progressively weakened, then the wayfaring man, though a fool, cannot err in the deduction that the South must prepare for a radical overhauling of its present agricultural policy. In an agrarian region this necessarily implies an important modification of the economic structure, and so of the social system.

But such overhaulings and modifications touching the lives of millions of people invariably mean trouble, unless they are handled with great energy, skill and intelligence. Take, for example, the minor item of the mechanical cotton-picker. This machine, if it has not been quite perfected, has been brought to the point at which its perfection is in plain sight; in the summer of 1936 unequivocal claims were being made that at least one device is commercially practicable. The moment it becomes as efficient, relatively, as was Eli Whitney's original cotton gin, the living of some millions of Southern farm workers will vanish. Not only will the cotton pickers of the Southeast be out of work, but the mechanical pickers will put the Southwest in position to produce a much larger proportion of the cotton crop. At present it seems likely that, with mechanical aid, cotton can be grown in the Southwest at materially lower expense than it can be grown, under any conditions, in the Southeast. Therefore cotton planters will also be out of work.

If this thing should come gradually, it might be possible to transfer these people to some other form of employment without any severe shock to the economic and social organization. But it will not come gradually. It will come with dramatic suddenness. Once the machine has demonstrated its efficiency, five years will be enough to establish it as a dominant factor. Then the South will have a fresh unemployment problem of appalling proportions on its

17

hands. The country recently has had only too vivid a demonstration of what a Pandora's box of evils a really large unemployment problem is. The mere cost of keeping the unemployed from starving is serious enough, but it is relatively insignificant by comparison with the bitterness, despair, disease, mental and physical stunting, crime, crazy radicalism and general social disintegration that accompany it.

Add to this the other and more important factors in the Southern problem, and it is clear enough that the present position of the region, far from being firmly established, is precarious in the extreme.

All this the facts presented in *Southern Regions* prove beyond dispute; and if it were all that they prove, then the book might well be classified as a textbook of despair. But there is another side, presented with the same clarity. If the evils that beset the Southern States are appalling, both in their magnitude and their imminence—and the cold figures leave no doubt of that—it is equally clear that for every evil there is a remedy, known, tested, reliable and within the reach of the South. If her needs are immense, her resources are enormous. If her perils are great, her bulwarks are capable of being greatly strengthened. If her problems are multitudinous, there is nothing *outré*, nothing unprecedented, about them; they are of a sort familiar to the race, and something is known about the way to their solution.

Time and again in the history of civilization regions, sometimes whole nations, have been overtaken by relentless doom. Nothing within the power of man could have saved Pompeii. Nothing within the power of its inhabitants could have saved the Persian empire of Shah Mohammed once Genghis Khan had begun his march. It is at least conceivable that nothing can save the western plains of the "Dust Bowl" now that the buffalo grass has been plowed under.

But the South faces no threat of this sort. Among all the threats that menace them there is no threat to the Southern States that cannot be met by prompt and intelligent employment of the resources available to the Southern States. It is not a problem of inevitable destruction, but a problem of waste. Waste can always be halted and frequently repaired. A modification of Southern economy, the main lines of which are plain enough, can correct the deficiencies of the region and multiply enormously its productiveness, not merely of trade goods, but of the satisfactions of life for the masses of its people.

There is a high road, as well as a low road, open to the Southern people. There is no insuperable obstacle in the way of their achievement of a position not merely as good as, but better than that they held in the early days of the republic. The civilization that produced Monticello and the Farewell Address, the oratory of Patrick Henry and the jurisprudence of John Marshall, the courage of Andrew Jackson and the integrity of Robert E. Lee is worth recovering even at the price of heavy labor; yet nothing is required for its recovery beyond energy intelligently applied.

To demand intelligence of twenty-five million people is, to be sure, to demand what is patently impossible. But, fortunately, to shape the polity of a nation it is not necessary to transform the entire population into philosophers. All that is requisite is intelligence in a relatively small group of leaders. Regardless of the form of government under which they live, the destinies of men have always been determined by a minority of mentally alert individuals. There is nothing unreasonable or unfair in calling upon the leadership of the South, first, to acquaint itself with the facts, and, second, to act intelligently upon the information. Yet if this is accomplished, there is no reason to doubt the swift return of the region to a level of civilization distinctly higher than its present level and probably higher than any that it has occupied before.

In the pages that follow there is a short and admittedly sketchy outline of the facts revealed in *Southern Regions of the United States,* followed by certain inferences that seem to be obvious. The purpose of this work is to present, not a condensation of the book, but a suggestion of what is in it, in the hope that thoughtful Southerners may be moved to go to the book itself to acquaint themselves fully with a situation that is of profound concern to every man who lives below the Potomac.

2. *The Waste of the Land*

THE STATEMENT ON AN EARLIER PAGE THAT THE South has thrown away ninety-seven million acres of land is startling enough, in all conscience, and yet it is an understatement. The figure represents only the land that has been ruined, or seriously damaged, by erosion. This is, however, by no means the only method of wasting land. Leaching is another method by which land is wasted. Destroying the fertility of the soil by overcropping is another. The South has been guilty of both of these practices.

Yet it is possible, nay, it is probable, that not erosion, not leaching, not overcropping, not a combination of all three represents the most serious waste of land. To devote an acre to one crop when an intelligent study of all the factors involved would show clearly that it might more profitably be devoted to a different crop is certainly a partial waste of that acre. If this sort of waste be taken into account, then the total waste of Southern farm lands mounts into truly astronomical figures.

In *Southern Regions,* an attempt has been made to measure all these wastes. It is certain that the measurement is not complete. The methods available were not sufficiently refined to reveal any but the more egregious forms. The last, and most prodigious item, for example, is not susceptible to exact measurement by any means available to statisticians. The most that can be accomplished is to indicate roughly its enormous extent. The statistics actually presented, therefore, may be accepted as the minimum, not the maximum, wastage that has occurred in the South.

Of all the forms of wasting land, erosion is the most spectacular and the most complete. Overcropping may be corrected. The damage by leaching may be repaired. The misuse of land may be discontinued. But a field once badly eroded is a field ruined for agricultural purposes. There are in the South today something like thirty million acres that have reached this stage of complete uselessness, and twice as many more that are already seriously damaged and plainly on the way to uselessness.

Erosion by water and erosion by wind are the two forms that are of economic importance. The South is touched by both, but wind erosion is confined to a relatively small area in the extreme west, while water erosion is concentrated in the region bounded by the Atlantic, the Gulf of Mexico, the Mississippi, and the Ohio and Potomac rivers.

This distinction between the eastern and western parts of the South in the matter of erosion is typical of a great many other distinctions. Indeed, it became clear quite early in the investigation that the answer to the first question, to wit, What is the South?, is a double answer. There are two Souths; or, to be exact, the South is divided into two distinctly different regions, one comprising eleven States, the other four. Texas, Oklahoma, Arizona and New Mexico are a region of their own, with an economy, a culture and an ethnic composition distinctly different, not from the Southeast only, but from any other region in the country.

To make this clear it is perhaps advisable to give a brief description of the method employed to determine what is the South. State lines mean nothing in a cultural survey, and even broad geographical divisions are not altogether reliable. Nevertheless, common observation reveals that the United States is divided into regions differing markedly from each other and more or less homogeneous within their own boundaries. The difficulty was to trace those boundaries in a way that would have any appreciable resemblance to reality.

The procedure adopted was to examine each of the forty-eight States with reference to each of more than seven hundred points, covering all the information for which a sociologist is likely to have any use. One of these seven hundred questions, for example, was, How much eroded and impoverished land exists in this State? When two States were found, for each of which the answer to this question was the same, or approximately the same, one point of similarity between the two was established. When the points of similarity became more numerous than the points of dissimilarity, then it was obvious that the two States were to be bracketed together. When it was found that a group of States had more similarities than dissimilarities, then it was clear that here was a distinct region.

The seven hundred points cover a tremendous range and variety of interests. The effort was to touch on everything that has any bearing on the cultural quality of the State. Here are a few, chosen merely to indicate how much ground was covered: acres of land, use of land; ownership of land by class; tenancy ratio and land harvest by tenants; kinds of livestock; value of farm property, implements, dwellings; taxes and decreased value of real estate; amount and distribution of farm income; growing season and precipitation; types of forest and timber; types of days per year; per capita tangible and true wealth; bank resources and deposits; postal receipts; corporation income; life insurance, building and loan; average teacher's salary; school revenue and expenditure; bonded and net State debt; manufacturing: distribution, value of product, earners, wages, horsepower, value added; waterways; production of coal, petroleum, building stone; apportionment of Federal relief; ratio of types of highways and gasoline to population and income; illiteracy by race and age groups; population per square mile; parks, monuments, refuges, sanctuaries; students by sex and by types of schools; physicians, hospitals; libraries; church members by sects; homicides and lynchings; location of dramatics; prisoners and offenses; radios; automobiles; stills seized; births and deaths by color and residence. Here are about forty, and there were six hundred and sixty more.

Of course the procedure was not as simple as this description would indicate. A blind man can see that some of these questions are more important than others. The total population of a State, for example, is more important than the number of illegal distilleries seized in that State. The statistics, therefore, had to be "weighted" by complicated mathematical operations familiar only to statisticians to balance this varying importance. Even when that was done, there remained one obvious factor of error that could not well be eliminated; this was the treatment of each State as a unit. There is a vast difference between the civilization of the region around, say, Brownsville, Texas, and the civilization of the upper regions of the Panhandle in the same State. The two are alike in hardly any particular. But as nearly all the statistics that form the basic data of the investigation are collected by States, this error, although its existence was recognized, could not be corrected without complicating and extending the work beyond all reason. All the boundaries are somewhat vague. For instance, both banks of the Ohio, where it flows along the northern edge of Kentucky, are very much alike; but it would be grotesque to assume, therefore, that Ohio, Indiana and Illinois are quite similar to Kentucky.

The check-up showed that, subject to these reservations, the United States falls into six fairly well-defined regions, two of which lie in what is traditionally known as the South. These regions do not correspond exactly to any well-known classification. Odum's grouping consists of the Northeast, including all the region from West Virginia and the Potomac River to Maine; the Southeast, bounded on the north by a line along the Potomac and Ohio—but excluding West Virginia—thence along the Arkansas-Missouri boundary, and extending southward to the Gulf; the Middle States, west of the Northeast and north of the Southeast; the Southwest comprising the States of Texas, Oklahoma, New Mexico and Arizona; the Northwest, extending from the Southwest to the Canadian border; and the Far West, comprising Washington, Oregon, California and Nevada.

Four items of this classification run counter to tradition. They are the inclusion of Maryland in the Northeast, along with New England, that of Missouri in the Middle States, instead of the South, and that of Louisiana and Arkansas in the Southeast, although they lie west of the Mississippi. But these classifications are justified by the facts. For instance, in a field of nearly two hundred indices referring to cultural development, Maryland qualified as Southern in only about twenty, and Missouri qualified as either Southeastern or Southwestern in no more. It may startle many and shock some Marylanders to know it, but their State is more like Connecticut than it is like Georgia, while Missouri, perhaps to her own surprise, learns that she is closer akin to Minnesota than to either Texas or Alabama.

Southern Regions, therefore, is predicated upon the premise, not one South, but two distinct regions, the Southeast and the Southwest. The Southeast comprises the States of Virginia, North Carolina, South Carolina, Georgia, Florida, Kentucky, Tennessee, Alabama, Mississippi, Loui-

26

siana and Arkansas, with a total population of a little over twenty-five millions in 1930. The Southwest comprises Oklahoma, Texas, New Mexico and Arizona, with an area somewhat greater than that of the Southeast, but with less than nine million people in 1930.

The Southeast is really the wasted land, for its social organization is vastly larger and more complex and social forces operate on a vastly greater scale there than in the Southwest. Erosion, for example, has struck both Oklahoma and Texas, but Odum says that of the ninety-seven million acres of eroded lands in the two Souths, probably three-fourths are in the Southeast. Secretary of Agriculture Wallace recently set at fifty million acres the lands so badly eroded as to be useless; if 61 per cent of this is in the South—as 61 per cent of the total erosion is—that means some thirty million acres of utterly ruined land. If we take three-fourths of this as the share of the Southeast, it means some twenty-two and a half million acres gone forever, as far as the uses of living men are concerned. When one remembers that the total land area of the State of South Carolina is 19,516,800 acres, one begins dimly to conceive the magnitude of the loss.

This cannot be set down, however, merely as loss. To a large extent it was preventable loss, which is to say, it was waste. The natural wealth of the Southeast is vast, but no region is so rich that it can afford to throw away more land than the equivalent of the State of South Carolina.

Nor does even the gigantic figure of twenty-two and a half million acres cover the whole of this waste. Odum estimates that another five million acres of lowland have been ruined, either by deposits of sand and gravel washed down from the hills, or by flooding and saturation due to the silting up of streams. This loss is especially heavy because much of the land affected was exceptionally good farm land, some of it better than the hillside acres that washed down upon it and ruined it.

There is no way of making even a rough estimate of the damage incurred by the silting up of streams and the conversion of what once were clear rivers into turbid yellow floods, but it is certain that an economic loss has followed in at least two ways, to anglers and to water-borne commerce. The sheer size of the earth movements involved is seldom realized. Measured in tons, or in cubic yards, the figures are so huge as to be incomprehensible and well-nigh meaningless. Only by examining a specific case can one begin to appreciate something of the magnitude of the movement.

It is a matter of historical record, for instance, that less than two centuries ago ocean-going vessels were able to proceed up the Patapsco River, at Baltimore, almost to Relay, Maryland. Today Relay is a matter of five miles from open water, and a concrete highway runs through cornfields where ships could sail in George Washington's lifetime. The Patapsco is a little river and its drainage basin is not large. By comparison with that of the Mississippi, it is as a postage stamp stuck on a barn door; and it is of trifling size compared with that of the James, the Cape Fear, the Santee, the Altamaha, the Chattahoochee, the Red, the Brazos, or a dozen other streams of the Southern States.

The muddiness of this water pouring down to the sea through a hundred rivers is the wealth of the South, draining away. To point out that it is estimated that 20,000,000 tons of plant food, potash, nitrogen and phosphoric acid, are thus dumped into the ocean every year means little; but it begins to assume significance when one links with it the fact that every year the Southeast spends $161,000,000 for commercial fertilizers, partially to replace these very things. All the rest of the country purchases only 2,500,000 tons of fertilizer a year; the Southeast purchases 5,500,000 tons—while at the same time, by the process of erosion, permitting 20,000,000 tons to drain away. In the great farming region of the Middle States, including such fabulously productive areas as Iowa, Wisconsin, Minnesota and Illinois, the cost of commercial fertilizer is 30 cents an acre per year; in the Southeast it is $2.71. The farmers of the Middle States are among the richest in the country; the farmers of the Southeast are the poorest. Need anyone wonder why?

Yet there is nothing inevitable about this loss. Much of it is due to the insistence of Southerners on farming land too steep to plow; but it does not follow that the only way to halt erosion is to abandon the land altogether. A very large proportion of it is capable of being put to uses actually more profitable than the cultivation of cotton, corn, or tobacco. Much of it would furnish admirable pasturage, and if put to that use would go far toward making up the

Southern deficiency in livestock. Some of it is potential orchard land, and practically all of it is capable of producing forest crops, lumber, wood pulp, cellulose.

There is yet another large proportion, however, which is not too steep for the plow and is perfectly capable of producing cotton, corn, tobacco or any other crop permitted by the climate, but which is being ruined by nothing in the world but incompetent husbandry. A farmer who drives his furrows up and down the slope, instead of across it, can ruin almost any land; yet so simple a precaution as plowing along the contour lines is ignored by thousands of farmers in the Southeast. Here is one instance in which the South loses by reason of its deficiency in technical skill. There are thousands of others.

Technical skill, however, is one form of wealth that can be supplied. The waste of erosion can be halted. If it were halted, in spite of the loss of twenty or thirty million acres, and the damage of sixty or seventy million more, the Southern regions still have enough arable land of fine quality to build an agriculture of incomprehensible value. Frightful as it is, erosion does not constitute the inevitable doom of the South. Great as are its inroads, it is as yet no more than a challenge to the intelligence and energy of the region; if they shall prove equal to the challenge, there is nothing in the way of an eventual recovery of more than has been lost. Nevertheless, to prove equal to it, they must know what they face; and they must know it soon, for another half century of waste at the present rate will cripple the region perhaps beyond hope of recovery.

Leaching, that is, the percolation of essential plant foods below the depth at which they are available to crops, is the curse of light soils, and is even more completely a problem of technology. It is usually associated with and really forms part of the larger problem of overcropping.

The evils of the one-crop system in the South have been recognized and denounced by writers on Southern agriculture at least since the days of Thomas Jefferson—indeed, there were laws against planting too much tobacco in the Jamestown colony long years before the "Mayflower" weighed anchor for its famous voyage.

Thus we face the curious fact that for much more than three hundred years the Southeast has been pursuing an agricultural policy that practically every observer has known was bad, and that many, especially within the past century, have realized is ruinous.

This is an anomaly, but there is another fact about it that is still more astonishing. This policy has been pursued although there is no natural compulsion toward it. There are areas on the earth's surface where farmers practice the one-crop system because, for climatic, topographical or geological reasons they cannot do otherwise. The Southeast, however, is peculiar in that it is capable of growing every crop that can be grown anywhere in the United States. It can and it actually does produce oranges, a tropical fruit, and barley, the grain with the most extreme northerly range. Everything between these two can be grown somewhere within its boundaries.

This fact has implications that lift the problem of South-

ern agriculture above the level of merely regional significance. *Possession of such a region is a great national
inheritance.* If this garden of America were cultivated with
the assiduity and intelligence that its extraordinary character deserves, not the Southeast only, but the whole
United States would be vastly richer, would have the
means of supporting an immensely more varied, generous
and splendid culture. Conversely, to have this region ruined
by being devoted exclusively to cotton and tobacco is a
waste of the patrimony of the whole nation.

Since all this is well known, and has been known for
generations, what terrific pressure has driven the Southeast into an agricultural policy that, instead of making it
the richest, has reduced it to the poorest of the six regions?
The answer is complex—so complex that Odum required
six hundred and three large pages to write it down—but it
may be summed up in the statement that, to date, our
economic, social and political polities have never developed
any adequate means of dealing with problems in the large.
We deal piecemeal with effects, rarely with causes; we are
perpetually treating symptoms, but seldom the disease;
our most far-sighted statesmen look forward for years
only, practically never for generations. Yet that, perhaps,
is less than just; there are plenty of Southern statesmen
who can see ahead, but none who can act reasonably in
accordance with what he sees. Their vision is acute enough,
but their statecraft is feeble and inadequate.

The difficulty is that a vast and ponderous economic
structure has been reared upon the basis of the one-crop

system, and any attempt to alter the foundation, unless conducted with great care and great skill, must bring down the whole structure. It would not only be unjust, it would be silly, also, to sneer at Southern politicians because they have not corrected this destructive agricultural policy. It is only in part a political problem; vastly the greater part of it lies clear of the field of politics, as that word is usually understood.

The difficulty is simplicity itself; it is the remedy that is so complicated that it has hitherto baffled human ingenuity. The difficulty is this: you have a farmer who has raised cotton for year after year until his fields are approaching exhaustion. The technical problem presents no perplexity at all. There are countless other crops that this land can produce in abundance, some of which would work wonders toward restoring its fertility—legumes, hay, melons, potatoes, peanuts, wheat, oats, rye, various sorts of truck, a tremendous variety of crops; or the land may easily be devoted to pasture, forest or vineyard with a reasonable certainty of success, as far as productivity is concerned. But then arises the unanswerable question—if he raises these things, where is he going to sell them?

His merchant is a cotton-buyer. He is trained in the handling of cotton. He has the market connections necessary to dispose quickly of cotton. He has the banking connections necessary to finance the purchase of cotton. But this same merchant might not have the faintest idea of what to do with a carload of wheat. In the first place, he probably has had no experience in judging its quality; and in the second place, he is not familiar with the market. Still less could he handle a carload of grapes or celery.

The Southeast, for all the recent development of industrialism, is still overwhelmingly rural, which means that the Southern farmer rarely has within reach an urban market sufficiently large to absorb great quantities of food and dairy products. There is agricultural land on Staten Island that is quite capable of growing wheat; but what Staten Island farmer would think of wasting his time and land and labor on wheat when only five miles away lies New York City, with its insatiable demand for celery, beets, beans, radishes and everything else that can be grown in a garden? The Danish farmers have commanded the admiration of the world by the intensive and intelligent way in which they have cultivated their land; but it must not be forgotten that their success is based largely on the fact that across a short stretch of water are sixty million hungry Englishmen, anxious to buy all that the Danes can produce.

The degree of industrialization that the Southeast has experienced within the last thirty years has ameliorated the condition of its agriculture appreciably. Around every Southern industrial center there are farm lands not chained to the one-crop system; and many farmers, given the chance to do so, have abandoned that system to their great prosperity and content.

A further development of industrialism is clearly desirable from this standpoint, although it is not necessarily true that it should follow its present line of development.

Southern industry, like Southern agriculture, is too highly specialized. Manufactures of cotton and tobacco account for a vast proportion of it. Birmingham's steel and scattered woodworking plants modify it but slightly.

But packing houses and tanneries to deal with vastly greater numbers of Southern cattle are plainly desirable. Cheese factories—there are only three in a region capable of producing enough cheese to satisfy the national demand —would naturally come along with them. To what extent the dry Southeast would tolerate the development of wineries is a question, but there is no question that the vine is one untapped agricultural resource of immense potential value. The fruit and vegetable canning industry is capable of some further development, although seasonal industries create social problems of their own.

The recent experiments of Professor Herty with slash pine encourage the belief that a large paper and pulp industry could be created in the South, and there is immense undeveloped wealth in mines and quarries. There is danger, of course, that enthusiasm for industrial development might convert a healthy regionalism into a narrow and poisonous provincialism. While a more diversified industry is plainly desirable, it does not follow that the Southeast needs all sorts of industry. A balanced economy is one thing, and a clearly beneficial thing; but complete self-sufficiency is another and by no means a clearly desirable thing. Why attempt to drag the hatters, for example, away from Danbury, Connecticut? They serve the nation very well where they are. Why try to take the manufacture of

35

typewriters away from Troy and Syracuse, or that of automobiles from Detroit? Long tradition has developed special skills in these localities; and typewriters and automobiles built below the Potomac would, at least for many
years, probably be worse, not better than those that the
Southeast can buy in the North.

The history of her industrial development up to the present indicates that the South, strong in textiles, especially
cotton, and in tobacco manufactures, and with increasing
strength in steel and iron, exhibits marked deficiency in
metal work requiring a high degree of precision. Watch-
making is not a Southern industry, nor the manufacture of
machine tools of the highest degree of accuracy. There is
no very compelling social or economic reason why she
should attempt to develop such industries as these. It is
possible to build a reasonably balanced economy without
them. The South will always produce cotton and tobacco
beyond her own requirements, furnishing a surplus for
export to other regions, or other countries; and this export
surplus will enable her to purchase those articles which
others by reason of special skills or other considerations
can produce to better advantage than she can produce them.

She does require, however, the development of such industry as can employ her own raw materials to supply her
own needs. Plows, hoes, rakes, shovels she demands in
tremendous quantities, and she has the iron ore, the coal
and the labor to produce them. Lumber and furniture,
brick, tile, roofing slate, building stone, lime, cement,
paper and cardboard, glass, pottery, wire, sheet-iron, paints

of certain kinds, glue, waxes, spirits, beers, wines, food of all kinds and clothing for twenty-five million people could all be furnished by the fields, quarries, mines and forests of the Southeast. All require processing to which the labor of an immense non-farming population could be devoted.

The development of regional industry primarily to supply regional demands does not of itself call for any tremendous concentrations of factories and population. More than that, the development of hydroelectric power plants and transmission lines is already so far advanced in the Southeast as to eliminate the necessity for concentration at points where the delivery of coal is easy and cheap. There are literally thousands of miles in the Southeast on any acre of which the establishment of a manufacturing plant is feasible from the standpoint of power, because the power is directly overhead. Further industrialization, therefore, does not necessarily imply any high degree of urbanization. This is true even when the industrialization develops in the form of relatively large units, as in textiles. Gaston County, North Carolina, has a hundred cotton factories; the county, taken as a whole, represents one of the greatest concentrations of cotton textile manufacturing in the country; yet Gaston remains predominantly a rural county. It should be even easier to avoid excessive urbanization if industrial development takes the form of a large number of small units—a cheese factory using local milk and supplying the needs of a county or two, a pottery supplying good ware to a trade territory measured in miles and not in States, a creosoting plant large enough to supply fence

37

posts for twenty miles around but without facilities or ambition to go after the South African trade, a quarry that disposes of the bulk of its building stone in the next town and not in Ottawa, even a nitrogen-fixing plant that can supply the Tennessee Valley, but not the Ganges Valley, too—this sort of industry the South needs, not only to supply labor to diversified talents, but, even more important, to enable its agriculture to shift from the one-crop basis. This sort of industry is needed to help put a stop to the waste of land.

Then, to purchase its coffee and tea, pepper and spices, watches, typewriters and microscopes, French perfumes, German music, California movies and New York drama, it may rely on a still large exportable surplus of cotton and tobacco, raised on land on which they are carefully and intelligently rotated with other crops. Imports of this kind are strictly consonant with a balanced economy. It is when North Carolina imports hay from Minnesota and apples from California, when Florida imports milk from Ohio, instead of from north Georgia and Alabama, that the system is plainly out of balance.

It is not its arable lands alone, however, that the Southeast has been wasting. The forests are another instance, in some respects even more spectacular. Once there were in the Southeast a hundred and twenty-five million acres of longleaf pine, one of the finest woods known to the building trades, as well as the source of naval stores. Today fourfifths of it is gone. The lumbering methods used in removing this timber from the Carolinas and Georgia make one of the most disgraceful chapters in the history of the nation. Vast quantities of it were never used at all. The felled trees were simply piled in heaps and burned. It is estimated that up to 1880 more trees were cut in the United States to clear land than to obtain lumber. Not only living men, but men in early middle life can remember seeing in the Southeast "deadenings" in which the trees were not even felled, but simply killed by girdling, that is, chipping away the bark in a circle at the base. The bare trunks were left standing to rot away, while the plowman threaded a tortuous and difficult way among them.

The lumberman who followed the pioneer farmer was as reckless and destructive. Methods no more intelligent and difficult than those employed for more than a century by the British in the teak forests of Burma might have removed the merchantable timber, yet left the forest; and every decade the lumberman might have come again to the same lands to harvest another enormously valuable crop. Instead, everything was slashed away ruthlessly; tops and branches were left scattered everywhere and fire swiftly completed the destruction. The result is that today only in Florida and lower Georgia and Alabama are any important stands of longleaf pine left.

The longleaf pine is characteristic of the low-lying coastal plain, but the hardwoods of the uplands have fared but little better. Within the memory of this generation the furniture factories of High Point, North Carolina, drew the bulk of their supply of such woods as oak and walnut from lands so close that much of it was hauled in on wagons. Today the same factories are buying oak in upper New York and in Canada. Forests were swept from countless hillsides and the land put under the plow, although it should never have been tilled on account of the steepness of the slope. Erosion promptly followed, and with it came the pollution and choking of the streams below.

Yet so rich was the original inheritance of the Southeast in forest lands that even this terrific waste has not worked its ruin. There still remain in the Southeast a hundred and ninety-eight million acres, or about 40 per cent, of all the commercial forest area of the United States. There are about seventy-eight billion board feet, or 43 per cent, of America's remaining supply of hardwood of saw-timber size, in this region, and a hundred and twenty-one billion feet, or 8 per cent, of the softwood.

Moreover, restoration of a considerable portion of the cut-over area is not impossible under an intelligent conservation policy. The great obstacle in the way of reforestation is not any hindrance of nature, but merely the taxing policy of the various States. A second difficulty is the lack of an efficient forestry service, particularly in the matter of preventing forest fires. Indeed, the chestnut blight, which wiped out one valuable timber resource, is the only visitation of nature, beyond the control of man, that has contributed importantly to the waste of Southern forest lands. All the other wastes were devised by man and should be subject to his control. Again, in the waste of its forest lands as in the waste of its farm lands, the South faces, not an inescapable doom, but a challenge to its resourcefulness and ingenuity.

From one standpoint it may be idle to discuss the remaining form of waste, the misuse of land. It is incredible that if the wastes of erosion, of overcropping and of destructive lumbering were halted, the society capable of such a feat would have much trouble in assigning land to its most profitable use.

However, some discussion of the misuse of land in its broader aspects may be to the point, because there is no doubt that this constitutes a part, and an important part, of the picture of the Southeast as it is today.

Overcropping in itself is patently a misuse of land. The plowing of steep hillsides that should be devoted to pasture is a misuse. The tillage of marginal and submarginal lands that should be devoted to forest is a misuse.

But the term may also be applied to a broader and more sweeping phase of the agricultural system of the Southeast. The most conspicuous example is the failure, so far, to develop a tremendously important dairying region, sweeping down from the already established Northern and Eastern dairying region, roughly along the line of the Appalachians, but including a large part of the Piedmont country of the Carolinas and Georgia, and extending into the Tennessee Valley.

Of course there is dairying in this country now. However, it is for the most part strictly local. What is contemplated here is the possible development of the dairy farm as the chief economic support of the region, in the sense that the cotton farm is the chief economic support of the coastal plain of South Carolina, but, of course, within reasonable restrictions. There would be no point in substituting dairying for cotton if another one-crop system were to be developed. The danger of that, though, is slight. Dairying by its very nature forces a diversification of the farmer's activities which cotton does not compel. Dairy farmers, as the country around Elgin, Illinois, has proved, may come to rely too exclusively upon dairy products and so lay themselves open to serious damage through market fluctuations; but it is hardly conceivable that a dairy farmer could ever become a one-crop farmer in the sense that the man who raises cotton usually is.

The reasons for envisaging the development of a great Piedmont-Mountain dairying region as a logical development of the future are both negative and positive, both geographical and social. Negatively, the index of contour of much of this land indicates that it should not be brought under the plow at all, but it is well suited for use as pasture. The rest, which may be tilled without excessive risk of erosion, is classified as corn and wheat land, but the character of the soil is such that it is highly unlikely that this region can ever compete on equal terms with the immensely productive corn and wheat land of the Northwest and Middle States. It can, and should, produce enough grain to supply the demand of its own towns, as well as farms; but there is no reason why it should attempt to raise a great export surplus of these crops. As for cotton, its cultivation is difficult in the uplands, and the yield is scanty. Orchards and vineyards, on the other hand, offer great possibilities to this region; both exist today, but both are capable of very considerable enlargement to the profit of the country; yet it seems unlikely that any of these things open the way to the region's maximum development.

If these negative considerations seem to force this territory toward dairying, there are two positive considerations that should exert a still stronger influence in the same direction. One is the nature of the land itself; the other is its geographical location. As for the land itself, it is excellent grass land, well-watered, with—except for a small area in the very high mountains—mild, open winters. Practically all the conditions that a dairyman might specify for an ideal dairy farm are here present.

As for its geographical location, it is surrounded on three sides by wide areas which nature has by no means equipped so well for dairying. The region immediately at the foot of the hills has already proceeded far along the road to industrialization. The tremendous textile manufacturing concentration of the Carolinas is, in many places, literally within sight of these hills. Here is a large market already developed to the east and one with a prospect of increasing materially. To the south is the Alabama steel-producing country, with Birmingham and its satellite cities; and beyond is Florida, a poor grass country, but an immense national playground, and a State that is already importing milk in huge quantities from regions farther to the North than the Appalachian *massif*. To the west lies

43

the Tennessee Valley which, if present experiments are even measurably successful, will presently be supporting a much larger population than inhabits it now; but even today it is an enormous market for dairy products.

Here, then, is an almost ideal dairying country, almost surrounded by millions of potential customers. Yet it is not at present a great dairying country. The conclusion is inescapable that here is an example of misuse of land on the grand scale.

Smaller and less impressive examples are to be found in large numbers. There is, of course, the question, mentioned on an earlier page, of whether the Southeast is not misusing its land in attempting to grow cotton at all. Certainly if the Southwest continues to produce larger and larger crops, it will presently become plain to the dullest that here is a case of misuse. If the present trend continues, it will eventually become economically impossible for the Southeast to continue to grow cotton, except on highly selective lands unusually well adapted to the crop. This will precipitate a crisis of proportions appalling to contemplate unless vigorous and intelligent action has been taken to prepare for it in advance.

The obstacles that lie in the way of development of a great Piedmont-Mountain dairying region are, in the main, those that lie in the way of a better agricultural system in the lowlands. They are economic, political, social—as contrasted with the dispositions of nature, artificial. There is, to begin with, the historical deficiency. The agricultural traditions of any region are of great importance, and here

44

they run against, or certainly not toward, commercial dairying. Closely connected with this, and of more immediate importance, is the deficiency of technical skill. There is a deficiency of available capital. All these deficiencies, however, are relatively minor. The really gigantic obstacle is simply the fact that the market available, while enormous, is a poor market. If the average income of the average Southerner in the lowlands were raised even slightly, then the problem of developing the uplands into a great dairying region would be enormously simplified.

The problem of waste of the land is basic anywhere, because the land is the nation's life; but in an agrarian region it eclipses all else, because waste of the land there involves waste of the whole people. The South is predominantly agrarian. It has always been so, and as far as the predictable future is concerned it will always remain so. Consider that the United States draws only 12.9 per cent of its total income directly from agriculture; then consider that in North Carolina, the most highly industrialized of the Southern States, 26.7 per cent of the State's income is agricultural. Indeed, such industrialization as has taken place so far seems only to have heightened the importance of agriculture as an income producer. Only Mississippi, with 46.8 per cent, and South Carolina, with 31.4 per cent, in the Southeast draw a larger proportion of their incomes from the farms than does North Carolina—and South Carolina, also, is highly industrialized, that is, as Southern States go. Of course it is not to be compared in this respect with, say, New Jersey.

It is no hyperbole, then, to say that for the Southeast checking the waste of the land is a matter of life and death. The Southeast no longer is pioneer country. No longer may the farmer, for every ravaged acre, bring a new acre of virgin soil under the plow. It is the misfortune of the Southeast that the pioneer's spirit of reckless disdain of the future has outlasted the pioneer's resources. The Southeast must live on what land it has. If that gets away, there isn't any more. It is getting away, with horrifying speed.

A subtle philosopher is required to decide whether it is worse to confront a problem whose solution is wrapped in impenetrable obscurity, or to confront one every step toward the solution of which is perfectly plain, but also extremely difficult to take. In any event, the second quandary is that of the South. The solution of the problem of the waste of the land requires only three operations, each of which is perfectly plain, and each of which is so enormously difficult to perform that it will tax the brains and resourcefulness of the region to the limit. But the fact worth bearing in mind is that none of these three operations is impossible. Difficult, yes; but not impossible.

One step is the correction of the existing deficiency in skill. To accomplish this the Southeast must somehow contrive to suppress its marked tendency toward xenophobia, the hatred of the stranger. This is essential simply because it has not in its present population enough technicians of the kind required. The training of its own technicians is a legitimate goal for the future, but it is a process covering years and the region cannot afford to wait. The Southeast

needs a tremendous importation of skilled outsiders—
Yankees, Germans, Danes, Dutchmen, Frenchmen, Ital-
ians, Swedes—anybody and everybody who really knows,
and who can apply his knowledge. There should be a new
army of invasion, comparable in size to McClellan's host,
but composed, not of infantry, cavalry and artillery, but of
engineers—civil, not military—foresters, agronomists, bi-
ologists, botanists, entomologists, plant pathologists, geol-
ogists, geographers, plant physiologists, soil chemists and
countless others.

Another step is to correct the deficiency in artificial
wealth. This sounds like advising the South to raise itself
by its bootstraps, but it isn't quite as bad as that. It is true
that the creation of artificial wealth is one of the goals of
the campaign, but the attraction of artificial wealth is part
of the process. The South, and especially the Southeast, is
going to have sharp and increasing need of investment
capital for the next twenty years, especially if it proves
necessary to shift the basis of the economy of the region
from cotton to something else. The preservation of the
credit of the region in the money market is therefore of
great importance. It can hardly be contended seriously that
the South has been scrupulously careful in this regard. Up
to 1933 there had been 1,261 defaults in county, city,
school district and other special tax district bonds in the
United States; of these 209, almost exactly one-sixth, had
occurred in the single State of North Carolina, and 558
were in the Southeast. The only State bonds in the country
in default at that time were those of Arkansas. It is incon-

47

testably true that the Southeast felt the onset of the depression years before it struck the rest of the country; it may be true that other regions, subjected to equally severe pressure, would have shown a larger number of defaults than they actually have shown; but it is also true, and every bond dealer in the country knows it, that a considerable number of Southern defaults, especially in county and municipal issues, were attributable largely, and some of them entirely, to archaic accounting and business methods and almost incredible incompetence in the handling of public finances. This sort of thing can be corrected; but unless it is corrected, it will present a formidable obstacle to the acquisition of that capital which the South must have if she is to succeed in establishing her economy on a sounder basis.

The third step is the correction of the deficiency in institutional services. Great strides have been made in this direction within the last thirty years, but much more remains to be done. County farm agents, public health services, rural libraries have multiplied amazingly since the turn of the century; yet the Southeast remains without a single university of the first rank, without a single engineering school of the first rank, and with only a rudimentary development of public services of many kinds. In this particular phase of the problem, however, the South may legitimately look for help from outside. Indeed, she has already received it in generous measure. The Carnegie Corporation has expended more than half its total in the South. The Rosenwald Fund for Negro schools, and the

48

earlier Peabody Funds for teacher training, have assisted greatly, while the Rockefeller groups have spent more than a hundred millions in the South.

When all is said and done, however, the waste of the land in the South is primarily a Southern problem which must be solved primarily by Southern energy and Southern intelligence. The rest of the country indubitably has an enormous stake in the preservation of the South, but the rest of the country has problems of its own which must engage its first attention. With all the good will in the world such assistance as it lends the South must be of secondary importance. If the South proves to be lethargic and stupid, it must inevitably pay the penalty.

But of all the regions in the country, the Southeast should be the last to find in this ground for lamentation and bitterness. Historically, it has cherished a strong, sometimes a fierce sense of independence. Its ability to maintain its own culture and its own traditions against the world has been its pride. If that pride has any justification, then the fact that the South must solve its own problem in its own way and with its own resources should not be regarded as an injustice or a hardship. An enfeebled nation might regard such a condition as a doom; but to a high-spirited people it is a challenge.

3. *The Waste of the People*

THE SOUTHEAST HAS DEALT WITH ITS HUMAN
wealth exactly as it has with the wealth of its soil—
part it has let slip away altogether, part it has failed to
cultivate at all, and part it has clearly misused.

Here, again, it is far from having a monopoly. There
is no country in the world that is not guilty, to some extent, of the same sort of waste. But here, again, the figures
for the Southeast run so inordinately high as to raise a
question as to the survival of the region at its present level
of culture; and this in spite of vigorous and by no means
ineffective efforts toward the conservation of human
wealth.

It has been the fashion in some quarters to assume that
the Southeast has remained almost completely inert in the
presence of its social problems. This is far from the truth.
A mere glance at the educational statistics of the region is
enough to dissipate the impression that the Southeast has
been indifferent or lethargic in this respect. The State of
Florida, for example, spends 5.76 per cent of its total income for school purposes, and North Carolina 4.38 per
cent; this is a larger percentage than is spent for similar

purposes by any other States save the Dakotas. Nor is the effort confined to primary schools. The Southeast spends .3 per cent of its total income for higher education, the highest percentage in the nation. It enrolled more high school students in 1930 than the whole country did in 1900, and there are more accredited high schools in this region than there were in the United States at the end of the century. Its present army of 60,000 high school graduates annually represents an increase of 500 per cent within the last two decades.

Such an advance is not achieved without vigorous and unremitting labor. Whatever else the Southeast may lack, it is not deficient in energy, although this is precisely the deficiency that superficial observers have most frequently attributed to it. The waste of its human resources is attributable to a wide variety of causes, but inertia does not figure importantly among them.

The counterpart of the Southern lands eroded beyond the possibility of any use is to be found, in the inventory of human wealth, in the item of three and a half million Southerners lost to the South. This figure, worked out by T. J. Woofter, Jr., is the difference between the number of persons born in the Southeast who are living in other regions and the number born in other regions now living in the Southeast. That this enormous tide of emigration represents a huge monetary loss is obvious, but the economists exhibit a distressing tendency to dispute among themselves as to its size. There are a dozen methods of calculating the value to society of a human life and each economist prefers his own.

Sir William Petty, the first to make an estimate based on something rather more valid than guesses, in 1690 calculated the worth of a man to England at £80, which, allowing for the alteration in the value of money, would be approximately $895 today. Two hundred years later Giffen and Farr, approaching the problem from different angles, increased that figure largely, Giffen to $6,712 and Farr to $3,356. In 1891 Nicholson, figuring in still another way, made it $13,985, while Marshall, in 1895, could see no more than $2,237 as the value of a life. Perhaps the most elaborate studies made up to that time were those of Barriol, a French actuary, who in 1910 published estimates varying for different countries. Barriol's figure for the United States, expressed in terms of the present dollar, is $10,561, which is a good deal closer to Nicholson than to Petty.

If one assumes, however, that Barriol was guilty of an error of more than 110 per cent—surely a generous estimate—one is left with a figure of $5,000 as the monetary value of a human being to society. Remember that the South has lost three and a half million of them, and it is apparent that this represents a loss in the order of magnitude of the national debt. It is probable that most living men, if called upon to cite instances of the most terrific spending within their experience, would mention the war against Germany and the New Deal expedition against the depression. The war increased the national debt by something over $25,000,000,000. The first four years of the New Deal increased it about $10,000,000,000, leaving out the soldiers' bonus as not attributable to the New Deal. But the South's monetary loss by emigration, at $5,000 a person, comes to $17,500,000,000—two-thirds of the cost of the war, or enough to pay not for four, but for seven years of the New Deal. That incomprehensible sum would pay for one thousand Department of Commerce buildings, or for one thousand, one hundred and fifty Louisiana Purchases. The most populous State in the Southeast is North Carolina, with 3,170,000 people. Emigration has drained away human resources equalling more than the entire population of the region's biggest State.

The irony of the situation is the fact that these people sought opportunity—and evidently found it, since they have stayed away—by leaving the region of the country richest in natural wealth and going into poorer regions. In the face of that fact, is it possible to doubt that there is something seriously amiss in the present economic and social organization of the Southeast?

Studies of the population of the Southeast have long ago made the whole country familiar with certain of its characteristics. Its bi-racial composition, of course, is its most conspicuous feature, and the first to meet the observer's eye. It is the most thoroughly American region in the sense that almost all its people are natives of this country. It is homogeneous in another way, too, for the racial origins of the bulk of the population are still the

British Isles and Africa, despite strong infiltrations of Germans in the Piedmont country and French in Louisiana, a slighter infiltration of Spanish along the Gulf coast and scattered enclaves of other nationalities here and there. In spite of the existence of numerous exceptions, it remains true that the typical Southerner is either Negro, or English, Scotch, Welsh or Irish. His culture is British; his religion, Protestant, predominantly Nonconformist, Calvinistic; his politics, traditionalist; his economic theory, individualist; his social code, a modification of that of Great Britain; his legal code, based on the English common law. There are important exceptions—the Code Napoléon, for example, is the basis of Louisiana law, and there are wide Catholic areas in Kentucky, as well as in Louisiana—but the exceptions do not modify the general picture radically.

What has been almost entirely overlooked, however, until Odum brought it to light, is the curious and extremely important fact that the people of the Southeast are young people, markedly younger than those of any other section. In 1930 more than 50 per cent of the people of South Carolina were under twenty years of age, and more than 49 per cent of those of North Carolina. Less than 8 per cent of South Carolinians and less than 9 per cent of North Carolinians were over fifty-five.

In the Southeast as a whole 45 per cent of the population were minors in 1930 as against something under 40 per cent for the nation.

The implications of this fact are far-reaching. In the

first place, it means that the Southeast has proportionately more children to feed and educate, and fewer adults in the prime of life to do it than any other region. It follows that in this region we should expect to encounter the greatest difficulties in the elimination of child labor and in the provision of the best type of public education—which is exactly what we do find. But add to this the fact that emigration from this region is very large and the problem takes on national significance. Emigrants from the South constituted nearly 4 per cent of the population of other regions in 1930; the Southeastern birth-rate continues high, and if emigration also continues, it is reasonable to assume that the proportion of Southern-born and Southern-trained people in the total population of other regions will continue to increase. Handicaps laid upon Southern children therefore may have far-reaching effects.

The typical Southerner, these figures show, is a poor man with many children. This must be borne in mind in estimating the value of any social program that may be proposed for the region. For example, it has an important effect on the public attitude toward such schemes as old-age pensions. In Kentucky 12.1 per cent of the people are over fifty-five years old—the highest percentage in the Southeast. Compare this with the 18.6 per cent of New Hampshire, the 17.8 per cent of Maine and Vermont, the 15.6 per cent of Oregon, and it is at once apparent that the problem of caring for the aged is much more serious in other regions than it is in the Southeast. This undoubtedly has something to do with the fact that in 1936 the Townsend Plan aroused less interest in this than in any other region.

The statement that the population of the Southeast is young might lead to the inference that it is therefore an enterprising, not to say reckless population, for enterprise and daring are commonly associated with youth. It is necessary, therefore, to emphasize the fact that the people of the Southeast are not merely young, but very young. When the population of South Carolina consists of 50.6 per cent less than twenty years old, and only 41.5 per cent between twenty and fifty-five, the people of voting age in that State are likely to think, act and vote, not so much as young people as, rather, the parents of large families; and enterprise and recklessness are not commonly associated with the parents of many children.

It follows, therefore, that anyone who would formulate a social program that will appeal to the Southeast must frame it to appeal to a population distinctly different from that of any other region not in more or less vague and debatable ethnic traits but in the sharp, definite factors of economic level and family responsibility. If two men obviously think differently the difference may or may not be due to the fact that one is a Celt and the other a Teuton; psychologists and ethnologists can debate endlessly over the point. But nothing is more certain than that two men will adopt different attitudes toward life if the first has one child and the second has seven, although both may be Celts or both Teutons. The typical Southerner's racial origin and cultural background are hardly as powerful fac-

tors in formulating his attitudes as the fact that he is a
poor man with many children.

Next in importance in measuring the situation as it exists
is the fact that the population of the Southeast is an agricultural population. Notwithstanding the immense growth
of industry within the last generation it is still an agrarian
region; more than that, it is still too strongly agrarian to
afford the variety of opportunities to its people that it
must afford if its civilization is to attain the highest possible level.

This assumption is sharply challenged by an important
body of opinion within the region itself. Even the relatively minor industrialization that has already taken place
has brought into the Southeast some of the characteristic
evils of industrialism. Bitter and sometimes bloody strug-
gles between employers and employes have occurred in
the South with what seems to be increasing frequency.
There are Southern factory towns where conditions of
labor and of living have developed a dreary sterility of
life comparable to the conditions in Lancashire which
moved British humanitarians to blistering denunciation a
hundred years ago.

These ominous developments have persuaded some very
alert Southern thinkers that further development of
Southern industrialism must tend toward duplication in this
region, if not of the slums of Glasgow, at least of the most
undesirable conditions that prevail in heavily industrialized
regions of the United States. They insist, therefore, that

the emphasis henceforth should be laid on the perfection of an agrarian culture, rather than on further industrialization.

The question, of course, is one of relative, not of absolute, values. The Southern Agrarians, needless to say, realize that a purely agrarian economy is an impossibility, and that if it were possible it would be as far removed from the ideal as the opposite impossibility, a purely industrial economy. The question is not, Should the South abandon its machines and factories, but, Is it now at, or close to the degree of industrialization that will afford its population maximum opportunity for the development of their capacities?

Part of the answer is to be found in the figures for interregional population movement. That movement still runs heavily against the South. People, in general, do not leave their homes and birthplaces without a compelling reason. The born wanderer is a rarity; it is beyond belief that the South has produced three and a half millions of them in this generation. Even rarer is the man with a highly specialized talent which can be exercised only in a special environment. An opera singer, an actor, a great base-ball player will naturally find restricted opportunities everywhere except in the largest cities; the Southeast has produced a considerable number of such specialists, but not millions.

The enormous exodus of its people from the Southeast is explicable only on the assumption that opportunities for people of ordinary capacity are limited in the South; and part of the explanation of that condition is found in the fact that the region is still overwhelmingly agrarian. In so far as natural conditions are concerned—soil, climate, rainfall, the existence of undeveloped land—the opportunity for farmers in the South is virtually unlimited. Unfortunately, this is not true when artificial conditions are taken into account—the economic system. Moreover, there remains the fact, basic but frequently ignored, that not all men are born farmers. Whatever may have been the condition of the race when Adam delved and Eve span, its subsequent history has conditioned a considerable proportion of it to occupations not directly connected with the tilling of the soil.

To force such people into agriculture is plainly a waste of humanity; yet there is reason to believe that the Southeast is so predominantly agrarian that it affords no adequate outlet for the energies of its people who are artisans, not husbandmen, by temperament. Therefore they leave in hordes. More than that—one is tempted to say, worse than that—there are many who do not leave, but who remain to become bad farmers—unhappy, inefficient, a drag upon the economy of the entire region and a point of weakness in its social structure.

It is arguable that such people would be still worse off in the slums of a factory district, although the proof is not immediately visible; but to assume that factories inevitably and necessarily connote slums is not merely to adopt a defeatist attitude, but to ignore demonstrated fact. Slums are the product, not of industrialism itself, but of its undesirable concentration—a concentration no longer necessary in view of the wide distribution of electric power.

As a matter of fact, such undesirable conditions as have attended the growth of the existing industry of the Southeast have usually developed in spite of, rather than because of topographical conditions. Very few Southern factories, especially those belonging to the textile industry, are cramped by lack of available building land. The industrial tenement is almost unknown in this region. For every one in existence there are probably a dozen communities inhabited by industrial workers which, as far as fresh air, sunlight, grass and trees are concerned, are almost ideal.

Without doubt, it would be detrimental in the extreme for the Southeast to develop tremendous industrial concentrations, crowding thousands of people into a few acres. But the present trend is plainly toward a system of widely-scattered factories and against congestion of population. The Tennessee Valley project, whatever may be said of governmental participation in its direction and financing, is physically in line with the more recent development of Southern industrialism in general, in that it tends to develop industrial plants scattered over a wide area. This sort of development has certainly not reached the maximum desirable for the orderly and symmetrical development of the region's cultural and economic potentialities.

Certain sinister features of industrialism in the South can neither be denied nor defended; which does not alter the fact that a further industrial development, on socially more efficient lines, might be expected to reduce the human waste that now characterizes the region.

The most conspicuous characteristic of the Southern population, however, is its bi-racial character. A group of eight million people of a different color from the other seventeen million is a feature so startling that it may be expected to attract more attention than perhaps it deserves.

It may be argued plausibly that one of the difficulties of the South is the fact that the Negro has been given more attention, as a Negro, than he deserves; and a good deal less attention, as a Southerner, than he deserves. Odum proceeds on "the assumption that the Negro is an integral, normal and continuing factor in the culture of the Southeast." The novelty in this is the word "normal." The very term, "Negro problem," introduces to most minds a suggestion of abnormality. Much of the thinking and writing on the subject, whether done by Southerners, by Northerners, or by foreigners, has, consciously or un-consciously, adopted the same point of view—the point of view, that is to say, that the Negro is something in the nature of an extraneous substance, in, but not of, the South, producing a condition abnormal, not to say path-ological.

Hence it has come about that the average man tends to regard anything touching on the bi-racial situation as in the field of therapeutics, rather than in that of prophy-laxis, something to be cured, rather than something to be developed. There is an adequate historical explanation for

61

this in the sudden, violent alteration of the Negro's political status at the time of the Civil War. Considering the terrific emotional stresses of the post-war years, it is hard to imagine how it could have been otherwise. Nevertheless, it certainly imposes no strain on credulity to suggest that this is not the ideal approach to the problem.

The range of medicaments offered to cure the Negro problem is immense. It runs from murder to enthronement. Immediately after the war it was seriously proposed by certain bitter Northerners that the Negro race be made sovereign in the South, and the white reduced to subjection; and ever since the war certain violent and lawless elements in the South have been attempting to cure what they regard as a malady by a process of extermination. Between these extremes men of innumerable grades of wisdom and sincerity have offered innumerable panaceas. But relatively few—and this includes Negro thinkers as well as white— have been able to disabuse their minds entirely of the theory of medication.

The inevitable result has been enormous waste of the Negro's potential value to the social structure. Not all of this is the fault of the white South, by any means. The hasty and ill-advised effort made in the sixties to project the newly-emancipated slaves into a political and social position they were not prepared to occupy has made any realistic treatment of their position extremely difficult. Not only did it create appalling prejudices, but it erected very substantial legal barriers against any direct and forthright approach, and forced Southern political and social polity into a sinuousness that has been productive of a thousand evils.

This is, however, water over the dam. What confronts the Southeast today is the problem of making the best possible use of eight million blacks. But this is no special problem. The same deficiencies that have wasted the energies of the white population are precisely the deficiencies that have handicapped the black, and any technique that will supply the one will supply the other. The Southern Negroes, like the Southern whites, lack capital, technical skill and institutional services. From this standpoint there is no Negro problem, only a Southern problem.

There is, of course, a very ugly and very refractory psychological difficulty born of that fecund mother of psychoses, fear. Originally it was the whites' fear of political domination by the Negro, supported by Northern bayonets. Later it was transformed into fear of the Negro's economic competition. These fears have produced hideous outbreaks of violence which, in turn, have filled the Negroes with a paralyzing fear of the ferocity of the white race. Together they are responsible for appalling waste of the energies of both races. This, not any marked economic differentiation, is the real Negro problem.

Yet there is much in the existing situation to indicate that even the intangible emotional complex that is the Negro problem will yield to a rational treatment. The basis of fear is being steadily reduced. In the first place, the Negro birth-rate, while fairly high, as measured by the national average, is not keeping pace with the white birth-rate in the Southeast. In the second place, within the last twenty years there has been a remarkable dispersal of the Negro population through other regions. New York, Chicago and Philadelphia all have larger Negro populations than any Southern city. In 1930 Cook County, Illinois, with 246,992, had the largest concentration of Negro population in the world, while New York, with 224,670 and Philadelphia, with 219,599, were not far behind. Seven other cities outside of the South have more than 50,000 Negroes and there are 149 Northern and Western counties with more than 2,500.

This has had the effect of transferring race conflict to other regions, but it has also had the effect of relieving the population pressure in the Southeast; and the lessening of this tension permits the belief that a more unemotional examination of race relations is not only possible, but is actually taking place in the region.

One may argue with something more than a mere color of reason that many of the difficulties that have arisen from the South's bi-racial composition are due to the fact that the situation has been studied too intensively in detail, and not enough in general. That is to say, countless projects for the alleviation of specific troubles have been advanced by whites, by Negroes, by Southerners, by non-Southerners, by wise men and by fools. Many of them, including some of the very worst, have been adopted and enacted into law by Southern legislatures, while others have been incorporated into the manners and customs of the people, which is to say, they have been made into law more rigid and binding than any statute.

But only comparatively recently has any considerable effort been made to treat the disease, rather than to alleviate its symptoms—or, rather, only recently has the idea begun to spread that perhaps there isn't any organic disease, but only a series of functional disturbances. Since the turn of the century the Southeast has been making real, if not always adequate, efforts in the field of Negro education. With the rise of the Negro in the cultural and economic scale, there has come also an appreciable reduction of the rigor of civil and social disabilities. And with both there is a strengthening belief that perhaps the traditional approach to this situation has been faulty.

This approach has been based largely on the assumption that there is something separate and apart about the Negro question that differentiates it from other questions. It has been too frequently assumed that here is a problem with only one aspect. From the standpoint of the whites, this one aspect is the threat that the Negro affords to Southern social organization and cultural development. From the standpoint of the Negroes it has been the threat that white dominance offers to the very existence of the Negro, as well as to his economic and cultural development. A tremendous proportion of the energies of both races has been wasted, on one side in exerting pressure to "keep the Negro in his place," on the other side in resisting this pressure.

This habit of mind still dominates much of the thinking

of the region and the waste continues. But there is another body of opinion, already important, and increasing steadily. This opinion rallies around the theory that eight million people ought to be an asset of enormous value, and that the real Negro problem is not how to render him innocuous, but how to get the largest possible value out of him.

Once this attitude is adopted, a good many Southern theories as to race become untenable immediately. A society that proposes to develop all the potentialities of any population group obviously must open to that group every opportunity that it is capable of improving. This does not necessarily mean any sudden, violent reversal of the white Southern attitude towards the Negro. Right after the Civil War the disastrous results of any such attempt were demonstrated with a clarity so frightful that it should be a guarantee against any repetition of that mistake. But it does mean that the Negro's demonstrated capacity in the professions, in business and in finance is to be recognized, not as a threat to white dominance, but as an addition to the total strength of the region. It involves a realization that every cultural, economic or social advance made by the Negro involves, not something lost to the whites, but something gained for the entire region, white and black alike.

Idealists have relied too much on the altruism of the white South in arguing for this or that alteration in race relations. No doubt the white South ought to treat the Negro justly because it is right to do so; but no doubt the white South is as fallibly human as the rest of the race and as feeble in its response to the categorical imperative. No man, however, needs constantly reiterated adjuration to do that which is patently to his own interest. The plain fact is that the Negro is, in Odum's words, "an integral, normal, continuing factor" in the social structure; the equally plain inference is that the stronger the Negro, the stronger the social structure. Let this once come home not merely to a few leaders but to the great body of the people and no argument will be necessary to persuade the South to open the gates of opportunity to the Negro.

Incidentally, this shift in attitude is not, and ought not to be confined to the whites. The more clear-headed Negroes realize that the American Negro has, to set off against his undeniable disabilities, certain tremendous advantages. He enjoys, for example, a high degree of political security; he is not exposed to the risk of invasion by imperialistic adventurers. Nor is he a colonial; the fruit of his labor is added to the wealth of his own country, and is not carried off as tribute to increase the splendor of some European capital. His standard of living may be lower and his death-rate higher than either ought to be, but both compare very favorably indeed with those of most parts of Africa. He has fallen heir to a rich cultural tradition, and in adapting it to his own emotional and artistic requirements he may at once enrich his own existence and make a contribution to the tradition. He has no small part to play in eliminating the human waste that is involved in racial conflict.

Reference has already been made to the relatively great weight that rests upon the Southeast in the matter of educating its countless children. To measure the full weight, however, one must take into consideration other factors than merely the number of children in the region in proportion to total population. For one thing, the maintenance of a separate school system for Negroes leads to some duplication of effort and increase of expenditure, especially in supervisory and administrative services and in higher education.

It is not, however, in the elementary schools that the educational system of the Southeast is most markedly wasteful and inefficient. It is true that salaries paid teachers in the elementary schools are frequently so low that the tendency is to drive the abler teachers out of the profession. It is also true that the onset of the depression caused many States and municipalities to make cuts in the school budget so drastic that they constituted, not economy, but gross waste. Such things, however, are not faults inherent in the system itself, representing nothing more than its ill-advised administration.

When one turns to the system of higher education, on the other hand, it is evident at once that there are elements in its very organization that make for waste. First and most conspicuous of these is the fact that here are twenty-five million people without a single university of the first rank. Neither is there a school of engineering of the first rank, nor a school of agriculture of the first rank. This means that the whole educational system lacks, first,

68

the institutional services that cannot be performed by any other than an institution of the highest grade and, second, the influence making for increasingly high standards that such an institution exerts.

Odum describes the condition of the Southern educational system as one of "immaturity." Certainly the essential economy of maintaining in so large a population at least one university of the very highest standard and technical schools of corresponding quality is not obvious to the immature. The tendency in the Southeast has been to regard institutions of higher learning, if not exactly as luxuries, certainly as dispensable. Southerners have been slow to concede the possibility that the excellence of the public schools of New England is attributable largely to the excellence of the universities there. The effort has been to build up a system of primary schools without first making sure of a continuous supply of highly trained directors of the system; and this procedure has been slow and wasteful.

It is not to be inferred, of course, that this policy was adopted of deliberate choice. When the Southeast first began to stir from the lethargy following a great and disastrous war, it confronted a condition and not a theory. There was an appalling illiteracy rate to be reduced at all speed and by such means as were at hand. In the Southeast, as in the Northeast, the business of higher education in the beginning had been taken in hand largely by the churches. The College of William and Mary, for instance, was at first dominated by the clergy almost as completely as was Harvard University. In later years it became the practice of each of the larger denominations to build in each State at least one college for men and one for women. In some States these institutions actually outranked the State university both in age and in importance. The program of public education that began about 1900 therefore encountered formidable opposition in the realm of higher education from these institutions, which naturally objected to being displaced. Many leaders who devoted their time and energy without stint to support of the public schools, not only failed to support, but actively opposed the establishment of adequately equipped public universities.

Unfortunately, none of the church colleges had the resources that were supplied to a Harvard, a Yale, a Princeton, to erect it into a university of the highest standing. The only organization strong enough to build a university was the State; but with most of the educated men in the population graduates of denominational colleges, it was difficult to organize support for a program frankly designed to lift the State university above all other schools. There was a moment, just before the depression, when it seemed that North Carolina was about to do it. Educational leaders cleverly took advantage of the enthusiasm of boom times to drive the University of North Carolina far up toward the rank of a first-rate institution; but terror engendered by the collapse of the boom defeated that hope. Financial support was withdrawn to an extent that made the university's assumption of the first rank impossible, and it has had much ado to maintain its standing even among the universities of the Southeast.

The lack of such a university, and of comparable schools of agriculture and engineering, has made the development of an adequate system of public education in the Southeast doubly hard. It is, therefore, a conspicuous example of waste.

Another is to be found in the multiplicity of church schools. Each denomination has felt the necessity not only of maintaining one college, and usually two, but of maintaining one in each State. The Baptists, for example, the most numerous of the sects, have colleges all the way from Virginia to Arkansas, but no institution in any sense comparable to the University of Chicago, which also began as a Baptist college. The Methodists have as many colleges, or more, and at various times they have threatened to concentrate on one great regional institution, as at Vanderbilt, at Emory, and at Duke; but no university of the first rank has been built as yet. Hitherto State lines have presented an insurmountable barrier to the development of a great privately-endowed university out of any of the Southern denominational colleges.

More important, perhaps, in its effect on the cultural development of the region has been the separation of the sexes. As in the Northeast, so in the Southeast higher education has been duplicated by the building of women's colleges; but the Southeast has been slower than the Northeast to convert them into liberal arts colleges, rather than finishing schools.

An argument can be made for women's colleges. Education is asexual, or ought to be. It is perhaps particularly important for the Southern girl, considering her environment and traditional inheritance, to learn somewhere in the course of her education that intellectual rivalry between women is possible. In coeducational schools it too often happens that the girl who is popular with the male students is regarded as a success, rather than the one who exhibits intelligence and industry. In a women's college this extraneous success is not so easily achieved, and the only road to recognition lies through intellectual effort.

But while the theory can be defended, it has no application if the women's "college" is really not a college but an institution for training in "domestic economy" or for dabbling in the arts, or a normal school for teachers. This has been the state of many so-called women's colleges in the South. The waste here involves not only the individuals of the present generation. It tends also to strengthen skepticism as to the value of higher education for women among women themselves, and therefore tends to perpetuate the waste in the future.

In any event, the maintenance of separate institutions for the sexes involves the duplication of many costs, especially in the administrative and disbursing departments. Without going into consideration of the desirability of separate education for women, it is a question whether the South, in view of the narrowness of its resources, on the one hand, and the greatness of its needs, on the other, is in position to afford the luxury of separate colleges for women. Nor is it necessary to debate the value of sectarian education to reach the conclusion that the South can ill afford to maintain as large a number of independent church colleges as it has now. Grant the desirability of having Baptist colleges, Methodist colleges, Presbyterian colleges, and so on—does it follow that it is necessary to have one of each in every State? Yet in many instances the larger denominations are maintaining, not one, but four or five institutions giving college work in the same State.

In the Southeast the problem of higher education, so far from being handled as a unit, is subdivided, first by the division between church and state, then by races, then by sexes, then by denominations and then by State lines. It is beyond belief that such fine subdivision does not involve some inefficiency, duplication of effort, lost motion— in brief, some waste. In view of the gigantic size of its educational problem, due to the great numbers of its children, the loss occasioned by unnecessary division undoubtedly is one explanation of the relatively slow progress the region has made despite tremendous effort during the past thirty years.

Some critics have explained the obvious deficiencies of the Southeast by the markedly religious character of the population—religious, that is to say, in the sense of church membership. This assumption, however, does not stand up well under the test of Odum's analysis. The truth seems to be rather that the characteristic religion of the region is more affected by its general culture than the general culture is affected by the religion.

In the Southeast 61.4 per cent of the total adult population are church members as against 54.3 per cent for the whole nation. Only the Northeast, with 60.2 per cent comes close to this region. Except in Louisiana and Kentucky, where Roman Catholics lead, the Baptists are the largest denomination in all of the Southeastern States, white Baptists in four States, Negro Baptists in five, with Methodists, white and Negro, coming next. With only 19.7 per cent of the adult population of the country, the Southeast has 33.4 per cent of the adult Protestant church membership, and 22.3 per cent of the total church membership.

The mere recitation of its numerical strength is proof that the church plays an important part in the life of the region. But its influence is rather toward the fixation of attitudes than toward the determination of programs. For one thing, the membership is divided into a large number of relatively small units, the average membership of the individual church in the Southeast being 137 as against an average of 235 for the nation as a whole. Moreover, the congregational organization of the sect strongest numerically, the Baptists, makes virtually impossible any concerted effort toward a specific social objective. The Southern Baptist Convention, being without ecclesiastical authority, cannot pledge any Baptist church to any specific program. The Baptists, moreover, having been for centuries a persecuted minority, are traditionally suspicious of any organic connection of church and state, a suspicion which they carry over from politics to secular affairs in general. In 1936 a proposal that the convention put itself on record formally as opposing certain notorious abuses, including the brutality of the chain-gang system and agricultural peonage, was emphatically rejected, not that any delegate had any defense of the abuses in question, but because reform of the social system was regarded as lying outside the proper field of work of the denomination.

Without doubt this attitude of the Baptists has had some influence upon the smaller denominations in the region. It does not prevent their clergy, including the Baptist clergy, from intervening informally in all sorts of political contests. The participation of the Methodist Episcopal Bishop Cannon in the presidential campaign of 1928, for example, was an epos of American politics which politicians of all parties not only remember but still discuss with awe and terror. Still, such excursions beyond the bounds of the realm of theology are usually individualist enterprises without acknowledged institutional backing. The churches did, for the most part, give their formal approval to prohibition, but their policy as a rule is to leave the formulation of social programs to other agencies.

This is frequently used as the basis of an indictment of the church in the Southeast, but it is by no means certain that it is an unwise policy. Considering the intense emotionalism that characterizes large sections of Calvinistic Protestantism, the participation of the churches, as such, in the formulation of specific programs might contribute more confusion than enlightenment. The participation of the faithful in the control of church colleges in the Southeast, for example, does not encourage the belief that the

75

church membership is a competent authority to pass upon technical methods and details of administration. The more successful colleges without exception are those over which the denomination does not attempt to exercise direct control, but delegates its authority to some representative body; and one of the weaknesses of the church schools is the reluctance of the denominations to delegate broad enough authority.

It is extremely difficult, therefore, to trace any connection between the deficiencies of the region and its unusually high rate of church membership. The attitude of the churches on social questions is determined by the general culture of the region, not the attitude of the people by that of the churches.

The rise of industrialism has brought to the Southeast a new familiarity with the various types of conflict known of old to regions industrialized earlier. If there is anything distinctly individual in the relations of labor and capital in the Southeast, it is the evidence that here is an obvious lag. The battles now being fought in the South are to a noticeable extent precisely the battles that were fought years ago in the Northeast and decades ago in England. The organization of labor in trades-unions, for example, is as far behind the Northeast as the Northeast is behind England.

Here is a form of waste that was, perhaps, inevitable, but that is none the less serious and none the less regrettable. Its existence is demonstrated by the very fact that in some cases it is being avoided. Here and there in the industrial regions one encounters an employer and a labor leader with a sense of historical analogy and a knowledge of the history of industrialism. In such cases some of the old errors have been avoided and some of the old conflicts escaped. Such men are exceptional, but their experience shows how heavily the region has lost by the lack of leaders conversant with the history of industrial conflict in other regions.

Southern industry is wasting time, energy and money learning by its own experience a great deal about labor relations that might have been learned from the experience of others. This is, however, a human rather than a Southern failing; we are all inclined to say, or at least to think, "It can't happen here," until it actually does happen. What is peculiarly Southern about the situation is the striking time lag between this and other regions of the country. This is not confined to Southern industrialism. It is markedly characteristic of the entire picture. The educational situation, for example, in many of its aspects is remarkably similar in the Southeast today to what was characteristic of the country as a whole in 1900. So are certain aspects of the region's agriculture, commerce, fiscal organization and social customs.

The point most worthy of emphasis in this connection, however, is that it is a decreasing gap. If most of the indices employed by Odum to measure Southern civilization show a distinct lag, most of those used to measure advancement within the last thirty years show an astonishing leadership. The backward region is still backward, but it has been catching up at an amazing rate. If it could contrive to reduce its wastes, human and material, there is hardly any aspect of its culture that could not soon be brought abreast of the rest of the country.

This is emphatically true of its industrialism. The men who founded it and built it largely on the basis of a paternalistic relation to labor are now old and are rapidly relinquishing control to younger hands. With them the era of individual proprietorship is yielding to that of corporate control, which has long ruled in the older industrial regions. The question before Southern industrialism is whether or not employers and employes in the Southeast will be able to profit by the experience of other regions.

This is by no means certain. Chambers of Commerce in some Southern towns are still advertising cheap labor and absence of union organization as advantages. In some localities there have been outbreaks of violence in industrial disputes in which labor resorted to sabotage and capital to the use of hired gunmen. The road is wide open to a repetition of the old error of ordeal by battle, with all its frightful waste of money and men.

On the other hand, there are the exceptional men referred to earlier. There is also a possibility that the governmental experiment in the Tennessee Valley may develop into a demonstration of a saner industrial order which will have an influence upon all Southern industrialism in other ways than by the distribution of electric power. The Southeast can avoid the greater part of the waste of industrial warfare. There is no assurance that it will do so; but it can.

A form of human waste which is probably destined to receive much more consideration in the future than it has been given in the past is waste of the people's leisure. It is already evident that technological development has presented the whole country with new problems of leisure and every indication points to the belief that these problems are more likely to increase than to diminish in the near future. It is, therefore, of great and increasing importance for society to equip itself to meet this condition.

The Southeast is markedly ill-equipped to deal with leisure. From time immemorial the development of the fine arts, and especially music, drama and literature, has depended upon the judicious employment of someone's leisure—sometimes that of the artist, as in the case of the most celebrated officer of engineers in military history, Leonardo da Vinci, but more frequently that of the patron of the arts, whether that patron be a Pericles, a Lorenzo de' Medici, a Pope Julius, or merely an appreciative and discriminating public. By contrast, it is hardly to be denied that the more corrosive and socially destructive vices are advanced most rapidly by the unwise employment of leisure. That sagacious and penetrating, if unconventional critic, H. L. Mencken, many years ago suggested the organization of a brass band in every Southern village as the most effective deterrent of lynching. His belief—pretty strongly supported by the evidence—is that an important contributory factor in many lynchings is sheer boredom, which makes any sort of excitement a welcome interruption of an eventless existence.

79

In any case, it is clear that there are wide areas in the Southeast where facilities for the profitable employment of leisure are entirely lacking, as far as institutional services are concerned. The individual is thrown back upon his own resources, and if these are inadequate, waste is inevitable. Certain forms of recreational organization, of course, are obviously not adapted to the region. To note, for example, that there is not a single great orchestra in the Southeast is beside the point. There is not a city in the region large enough to support one. As much may be said of the lack of theaters, which, since the rise of the movies, have been more and more confined to the largest cities in the country.

But dozens of Northeastern and Middle States villages have proved that no great population is needed to support admirable singing societies, and even well-trained choruses. Symphony orchestras may be beyond the means of the South—although at least one, partially supported by Federal government funds, has done respectable work in North Carolina recently—but small ensembles do not require the backing of millionaires. Their scarcity in the region is evidence of its failure adequately to prepare for the use of leisure.

The monumental proof of this failure, however, is the situation with regard to books and libraries. Take any sort of index you please, and the deficiency of the Southeast is marked. There are more than six hundred counties in the Southeast without a public library. Compare this with nineteen in the Far West, forty-six in the Northeast and eighty-five in the Middle States. The American Library Association has fixed as the standard of income for libraries—that is to say, the amount necessary to furnish really adequate service—one dollar per capita. The Far West spends $1.08; the Southeast, 16 cents. The same authority estimates that a public library really well used will circulate five books a year for each person in the area it serves. Again the Far West does a little better than this, while the libraries of the Southeast circulate seventy-seven hundredths of one book per capita. Again, it is estimated that in a community where reading habits are well established about 30 per cent of the total population will be registered as users of the library. The Far West has 29.9 per cent, the Southeast 5 per cent.

The situation regarding periodicals is similar. In the whole country there are 3.20 people for each copy of a daily newspaper issued. In Mississippi there are 18.11, in South Carolina, 12.44, in Arkansas, 12.29. In the whole country for each copy of forty-seven leading magazines issued there are 3.97 people. In Mississippi there are 12.49, in South Carolina, 10.81, in Alabama, 10.76. It brings to mind the melancholy dictum of J. Gordon Coogler, the Alabama poetaster:

Alas for the South! Her books have grown fewer,
She never was much given to literature.

The curious fact is, however, that Mr. Coogler was wrong. It remains true that the South's books are few, much below her needs. But to say that they are growing fewer is altogether false. On the contrary, here is another instance of a lag that has been reduced notably within the last generation. In the Southeast are four of the thirteen States that have State Library Commissions. The Southeastern and Southwestern Library Associations, in conjunction with the American Library Association and four great non-Southern foundations, have been doing notably successful work in establishing library service where it never existed before, and in extending the effective range of existing libraries.

Remarkable as this work has been, however, it is proceeding too slowly to keep pace with the increasing need. Granting that the seven years following 1929 were abnormal times, presenting an unemployment problem out of all proportion to what may be expected in the future, the fact remains that both technological innovation and social organization tend toward giving the population an increasing amount of leisure. Facilities for its proper utilization therefore assume an increasing importance. This increased leisure may be equally effective in contributing to a raising or lowering of the level of civilization. The direction that the Southeast will take unquestionably depends to no small degree upon her success or failure in supplying her people with the things necessary to assist them in avoiding waste of this leisure.

The foregoing is not an exhaustive list, but it includes the principal forms of human waste that Odum's inventory reveals in the Southeast. There are dozens, perhaps hundreds, of minor wastes easily traceable by the statistician; but these are the greatest.

Like the waste of the land, the waste of the people in the Southeast is, in practically every form it takes, avoidable and remediable. This is not to be effected by any panacea, to be sure. The problem is complex and not to be solved by the application of any neat and simple formula. But while it is complex, it is not obscure. Every phase of it has been encountered before somewhere in the world, and somewhere a remedy has been found and applied. The Southeast is under no compulsion to sail uncharted seas in search of remedies for the evils that beset her. Her business is to apply the known, the tried, the tested; although it does include the application of some things hitherto unknown in her experience, they are all sufficiently well known in other times and other climes. Much of it, indeed, is so obvious that even mention of it is justified only by the fact that so far it hasn't been done. And yet, all experience goes to show that one of the most difficult aspects of the conduct of human life is precisely the application of common sense to every situation. It would be fatuous to assert that the task lying before the Southeast is an easy one. But it can be done.

4. *The Direction of the Answer*

IN VIEW OF THE INTENSE SECTIONALISM OF MANY
Southerners it may seem fantastic to suggest that the
first duty of the inhabitants of the Southeast in the present
situation is to learn that there is a South.

Nevertheless, this is the case. In the past there may
have been a South in the form of the Confederacy, although historians have produced much evidence to dis-
prove the assertion. There is reason to believe that the
Confederacy failed precisely because it never was an entity,
but consisted of a loose aggregation of States which frequently pulled against each other. In the present there are
those who believe in the existence of the South as a sort of
mystic entity of souls bound by belief in a common tradition. But even with these it is a matter of one's birthplace
and one's manners and customs, with, perhaps, the addition of climate. It is a psychic, rather than a physical
phenomenon.

What is almost entirely lacking is appreciation of the
existence of an actual, material, tangible South, consisting
of land, water and people, and bounded by lines which a
flesh-and-blood surveyor can trace with wooden stakes

84

driven into genuine dirt. To be a little more exact, we need to realize that there are two such Souths, a Southeast and a Southwest, neither a psychic entity, but a material manifestation, existing in space and time and subject to description by the ordinary weights and measures used every day in commerce.

What most Southerners mistake for the Southeast is in reality North Carolina, or Tennessee, or Florida, or Arkansas, surrounded by a group of other commonwealths with which it has more or less vague and tenuous, and altogether optional, relations. Among such Southerners there is hardly any greater heresy than to suggest that Alabama is really a part of Georgia, or that South Carolina appertains to Tennessee. Yet the fact is that, out of seven hundred characteristics, each Southeastern State is a part of all the others in more than three hundred and fifty, and separate from the others, distinctive and individual, in only a minority of these characteristics. To be Virginian, that is to say, is to be more Georgian than non-Georgian. To be Arkansan is to be more Kentuckian than Texan.

In nothing else are the Southeastern States more closely bound together, more completely merged, than in the waste of their resources, economic and human; and as the waste is a unit, so must the effort to check it be unified, if it is to be effective.

This does not imply that geographical and political lines must be erased from the map, but it does imply that they must be partially erased from the minds of the people. There must be a realization that the imaginary line that separates the two Carolinas, for example, is not a boundary ordained of God, eternal and immutable as the Appalachian *massif,* but merely a convention agreed upon for administrative purposes and to be disregarded whenever the welfare or convenience of the people may require. On the other hand, it is requisite, also, that Marylanders and Virginians realize that they are separated by more than the Potomac River—that here, or hereabouts, is a genuine boundary line, dividing cultures that are oftener unlike than alike.

This is the meaning of regionalism—this realization that the United States is divided, indeed, but not into forty-eight entities. The number is closer to six. Within each of the six there are problems soluble only by regional effort. The problem of waste within the Southeast is such a problem.

As it is set down on paper this sounds beautifully simple, but its application will be enormously complex and difficult. Indeed, it may be said with confidence that if the Southeast were able to make itself think regionally, all its other problems would be solved with an ease that would astonish the world. From the foundation of Jamestown we have been accustomed to think otherwise, and mental habits cultivated for more than three hundred years are not to be eradicated lightly and easily.

That very technology which has intensified some of the problems, however, is at the same time of great assistance in breaking down intellectual provincialism. The increasing ease of transportation and communication has already lowered, where it has not entirely removed, the ancient barriers. State lines mean little to a motorist, and still less to an aviator. There is small room for doubt that the mental horizon of most Southerners has been set back appreciably within the last generation.

Regardless of this, however, it is essential to the discussion to assume that Southerners are capable of thinking regionally. To admit that they cannot do so would be to yield the question in advance and make this discussion entirely meaningless. Assuming, then, that the intellectual readjustment can be, and will be, effected, what are the logical first steps for Southerners to take toward the elimination of the Southeast's deficiencies and the checking of its wastes?

There is no answer, if one insists that the answer shall take definite and specific form. No man is wise enough to say that a statute containing such and such clauses should be enacted by such and such legislatures, or that a corporation empowered to do thus and thus should be formed by identified persons. One of the worst mistakes the Southeast could make would be to assume that her problems can be solved by the conventional idea of "planned economy," that is to say, a cut-and-dried program providing for certain actions to be performed on specified dates. The Southeast needs a planned economy, to be sure, but not that kind. Almost the only thing that can be said about the situation with absolute finality is that no one understands all its implications, and that no one can predict what may develop out of some of the existing situations. Hence the only certainty about any detailed program is that it is certain to be wrong.

But while the making of blueprints at this time is out of the question, it does not follow that it is impossible to survey the situation and to determine which are the logical points on which to make the first assault. This is, indeed, not merely possible, but essential; the adoption of a hard-and-fast list of specifications, foolish as it would be, is only the second most disastrous folly into which the region might stumble. Worse than that would be to adopt no program and make no effort.

In Odum's opinion, the problems facing the Southeast fall naturally into four classifications, or four groups. Each group includes a wide variety of problems centering around (1) agriculture, (2) industry, (3) politics and government, and (4) institutions of learning including the whole field of higher education and that of original investigation, as well.

If one accepts this classification, there is not much doubt about which of the categories demand first attention. The South is agrarian, and will almost certainly remain so throughout the predictable future. As long as her agricultural policy remains faulty, the basis of her economy will remain weak. As long as her farm population remains below the highest cultural level it is capable of attaining, the culture of the entire region will remain deficient. The establishment of Southern agriculture on a socially, as well as financially profitable basis is therefore a problem that must be in process of solution before it is worth while even to attack the others.

However, any successful attack on the large group of problems that center around agriculture will require technical skill of a high order. Whence are the required technicians to come? They can be imported from other regions, and doubtless a certain number will have to be imported; but the importation of technicians, even when it is practical at all, inevitably involves some waste. There are always, in every region, special considerations, psychological and historical, with which a newcomer to that region must familiarize himself before he is capable of doing his best work. Technicians Southern-born and Southern-trained would possess the initial advantage of thorough familiarity with these special considerations. Moreover, even imported technicians require library and laboratory facilities which at present are not available in the Southeast. Finally, it is idle for the region to expect the universities of other regions to undertake all the original investigation that is urgently required by the Southeast.

For these reasons it is evident that the fourth group of problems takes priority along with the first. This insistence upon the desirability of Southern men for Southern jobs sounds a bit like the foolish provincialism which has long cursed the region and which insists that it is better to have a bridge in Georgia built by a bad engineer from Georgia than by a good one from Massachusetts. That sort of thing, of course, is neither economy nor patriotism. It is, in fact, a betrayal of the State by churlish stupidity. But as between two men of equal ability and identical training, there is a perfectly sound reason for giving the Georgia job to a Georgian rather than to a man from Massachusetts; it is the presumption that the Georgian is already acquainted with Georgia labor, climatic conditions and other special, local circumstances that may have a bearing on the speed and efficiency with which the work will be done, while the other man would have to spend some time learning these things after his arrival on the job.

As far as the natural sciences are concerned, it may be argued plausibly that the Southeast's need for at least one first-rate school has reference to the postgraduate work done in such schools rather than to the instruction of students. There is no imaginable reason why a metallurgical chemist, for example, trained in Vienna may not work as well in Birmingham as if he had received his education in the Southeast; but there is every reason why a Viennese school should not be expected, or asked, to devote its laboratories and much of the time of its best men to research in the problems of metallurgical chemistry presented by the ores of the Southeast. The same reasoning applies to all the other natural sciences. While undergraduate students in most of these sciences may be trained as well, except for the item of expense, in other regions as at home, the Southeast needs badly the services of the sort of research men that are inevitably attracted by a scientific school of the highest standard.

As regards the social sciences, however, the case is different. In these the special, local circumstances nearly always have a more direct and more powerful influence upon the work itself than is the case in the natural sciences. Here the historical background, the traditional attitudes, the social and political relationships are as important to the scientist as geological formations are to the bridge builder; with the difference that whereas any geological formation to be found in the Southeast is duplicated, or closely paralleled, somewhere else in the world, the psychological composition of this region, like that of every other comparable area, is unique. It is undeniable that many social scientists trained in other regions are doing successful and sometimes brilliant work in the Southeast today; but it is probable that most of them would admit that had training of the best type been available in the region where they are doing their work, it would be advantageous to have been trained there.

The case is doubly strong when one turns to consideration of original investigation in the social sciences. Here the very material is different from that with which investigators in other regions work. The biologist may be able to detect no difference whatever between *Bacillus typhosus* in Maine and in Alabama; but the sociologist knows that the prime causes of juvenile delinquency in Chicago are not necessarily anything like those that fill the reformatories in Mississippi. To say that the Southeast has great need of its own investigators in the social sciences is not to disparage the work done by scholars in other regions. It simply has no bearing whatever on that work. It is only recognition of the obvious fact that the history of Massachusetts is not the history of North Carolina—nor the economics, the sociology, the jurisprudence, nor even, in important respects, the psychology, in the same sense that the physics, say, of one point in the world is the physics of every other point.

The second and third groups of problems, those centering around industry, and those around politics and government are pressing, indeed, but demand immediate consideration somewhat less imperatively than those surrounding agriculture and institutional services. As the first and fourth group are attacked, it seems reasonable to believe that the other two will become increasingly important; certainly the reëstablishment of agriculture is intimately allied both with industry and with politics and government, while the field of education covers all three. The problems of the Southeast may fall into groups, but not into compartments. They are all inextricably involved, yet, roughly, very roughly, speaking, priority belongs to those named.

What, then, is to be done? Granting the necessity of action, granting the grouping of problems, granting the priority of agriculture and education, what is the actual first step?

The first step is to disabuse our minds of the belief that any miracles can be, or ought to be performed. One is almost afraid to employ the word "planning" because of the aura of necromancy with which it has lately become surrounded in the minds of the people; yet planning used to be regarded as a sane and sensible procedure, having no association whatever with wizards and warlocks, alchemy and Utopianism. Today to hint at a planned economy for the Southeast brings to many minds a picture of an economic, political and social upheaval as vast and disturbing as the Russian Revolution. Nevertheless, if anything of appreciable value is to be accomplished in the Southern regions, it must be preceded by a lot of head-scratching, a lot of calculating and figuring, the making of many diagrams, maps and tables. And what can that be called but planning?

Against the instantaneous-miracle idea Odum sets up the suggestion of not less than twelve years' labor. Relegate Jack to the fairy tale where he belongs, and waste no tears if the beans we plant tonight have not grown up to heaven by tomorrow morning. The first step for Southerners is to accept the inevitable and prepare for a long pull.

The next step is not the introduction of any new activities, but a more compact and efficient organization of those already in progress. This involves getting over a terrific psychological hurdle, invisible, but none the less formidable. It consists of the imaginary lines that bound the States.

The average man, if he were to stop to list it, would probably be amazed by the amount of social planning already under way in the Southeast. There is a State Planning Board in all of the States but two. The Tennessee Valley Authority is a gigantic experiment in social planning. The Agricultural Adjustment Administration, the

Resettlement Administration, the Civilian Conservation Corps, and so on, were others. But the evidence indicates that the State Planning Boards are too small and the national ones too big to operate with maximum efficiency. There is need for something in between, something that will not be cramped within State lines, nor sprawled all over the continent, but will operate within a region that is a natural unit.

The TVA suggests the model. It operates within a natural region regardless of State lines. But the TVA will not serve the purpose without radical modifications, because it is not inclusive of all the energies of the region. It is a Federal agency, and what is needed is a regional agency. It is a political agency, and what is needed is a social agency. It is predominantly economic, and what is needed is something more broadly human.

What are the forces that the Southeast has available to attack these problems? There are States, counties, cities, towns; churches, colleges, schools, lodges; Federal grants, philanthropists' gifts, foundations' allocations. All of them are active now, all of them more or less effective, but their efforts are headed up nowhere, they frequently pull against each other, overlap, duplicate effort and expenditure. The same amounts of energy and money, if properly organized and directed, would get far greater results; and if results began to show, it would be easier to get more money and more labor.

The logical first step for the Southeast, therefore, is to collect the forces it has already in the field and set them all pulling in the same direction. This obviously cannot be accomplished without some sort of headquarters, somewhere. Eleven different State capitals obviously cannot serve, and Washington is too far away and too busy with the problems of all the rest of the country. The Southeast needs a central directing authority. Call it anything you like—the name is of no consequence. If Regional Planning Board frightens some people by conjuring up visions of Marxism and bewhiskered Bolsheviki, call it the Young Men's Heathen Association, or the Bombay Bicycle Club; it will operate as well under one name as another.

The point is, the Southeast needs some central authority from which it may obtain exact and comprehensive information supplemented by intelligent direction. Take the problem of farm tenancy, to select the first one that comes to mind. Its dangers and difficulties are recognized everywhere. There is hardly a newspaper, or a political orator, or a preacher in all the South that is not frequently and fervently eloquent on the subject. No economist has failed to give it some consideration and few have refrained from writing a book about it. Yet the amount of precise, comprehensive and relevant information that is available on the subject is shockingly small. It is being attacked everywhere and in all sorts of ways, except one way, to wit, systematically.

There is no simple, single solution of the problem of farm tenancy. Hence the intelligent thing to do would be to have some central authority lay off areas in various parts of the South, apply one solution here, another there and check the results carefully. With a dozen such experiments in progress and under sharp scrutiny, the chances of evolving practicable solutions for the manifold forms of this problem would be enormously increased; and—which is of equal importance—methods that were manifest failures could be avoided in the future.

Farm problems other than tenancy which plainly require some concerted form of attack include the provision of an adequate credit system; some readjustment and redistribution of present crop-land uses, with some new crops and a very large increase in ratio of food and feed crops; some method of raising the standard of consumption, not of the rural population only but of the city dwellers as well; encouragement of interregional exchange and trade; an economic reorganization that will enable the farmer to use his cash to purchase other things than fertilizer, feed and food; an improved marketing system; more convenient and attractive farm homes; some rearrangement of the population to make the best use of the land, but not wholesale retirement of land and shifting of population; some more effective means of stimulating agricultural exports.

Obviously, there is no human being alive wise enough to lay out a detailed program for accomplishing all these aims. In the first place, as regards many of them, there is simply not enough information in hand on which to base a really intelligent approach to them. Above all, there is next to no reliable and adequate information about their *relations* to each other, and to the region as a whole. Nothing is gained, from the regional standpoint, by solving one problem through methods which create two new problems. It would profit the Southeast nothing to rescue the agriculture of, say, South Carolina, by methods which would ruin the agriculture of Alabama. The AAA ran headlong into this error in the early days, when its cotton restriction program turned so many Southeastern farmers to raising potatoes that they wrecked the potato market and necessitated a potato-control act. An indispensable factor of any successful social program is balance, and balance is attainable only through consideration, simultaneously, of all the factors in the situation.

This is what justifies giving priority, along with agriculture, to the development of institutional services. Any regional planning, to have the faintest hope of success, must be based, not on guess-work, but on full, precise and accurate information. Raw data, such as are collected by the various State and Federal statistical agencies, are not enough. Such data must be treated scientifically before they are useful for the purpose, and the working of raw data into assimilable information is a function of universities.

Here, again, the immediate problem is not the creation of new machinery, but the creation of an organization capable of using to best advantage the existing machinery. While the Southeast has no university of the first rank, it does have a number of institutions capable of doing, and actually doing, excellent field work in the social sciences. But here, again, the work is unsystematic and disorganized for lack of recognized central direction. With one really first-rate university correlating their efforts, a dozen South-eastern institutions of lesser rank would immediately become many times as effective as they are now.

On this problem the South may with propriety appeal for outside assistance. There is not even a TVA model to serve as a guide in this case. To the vast majority of the population, a great university means scores of large buildings, thousands of students and a successful football team. The laboratories, the library, the publications, and the freedom of its ablest men both from a crushing teaching load and from financial straits mean little, if anything.

There are, however, in the country a number of large foundations dedicated to the advancement of learning. Most of them are well aware that the problem of the waste of the Southeast in its larger aspects is a national problem, and therefore easily within their province. Many of them have already evinced an extremely active interest in the region, and such progress as has been made in higher education in the Southeast is to a large extent attributable to this interest. The Carnegie Foundation, for example, has spent more than half its funds in the South; more than a hundred million dollars of Rockefeller money has gone into Southern institutions; the Rosenwald Fund has chosen the South as its particular field.

There is every reason to believe, therefore, that the scarcity of immediately available capital is no insuperable obstacle to the establishment in the Southeast of institutions—not universities, alone, but engineering and other technical schools—of the highest grade. What is needed is a concentration of effort, an organization of the energies of the region; but this naturally presupposes some mitigation of local institutional jealousies and the conception of an institution as regional, rather than local.

Is this impossible? Well, it has been successfully accomplished elsewhere. Is Harvard a Massachusetts institution? Is Yale the property of Connecticut? Does Princeton serve New Jersey alone? Is the Johns Hopkins dedicated to the exclusive use of Maryland? If the people of the Northeast are capable of admitting the regional preëminence of their great institutions, surely an equally intelligent view is not beyond the capacities of the people of the Southeast. Yet if it could be demonstrated to the world that any existing institution in the Southeast, or a new one, really commanded the confidence of the region as a whole, there is every reason to believe that the great foundations would see to it that it was not choked into helplessness by lack of funds.

"Planning for a reconstructed agriculture in the Southeast," says Odum, "will require rare strategy, skill, boldness." This is putting it conservatively. It will require—to be quite successful—unprecedented strategy, skill, boldness. But the stake is even more immense than the difficulty. The Southeast is capable of becoming quite literally the garden of the world. But if the program were only partially successful, if the region exhibited no more strategy, skill, boldness than has been displayed by the people of, say, southern California, the wealth of the region would be increased by a staggering proportion and it would be capable of sustaining a civilization as fine as any the world has ever seen—in some respects, finer than any that has been seen heretofore.

The group of problems centering around Southeastern industry has been described here as of less immediate concern than those surrounding agriculture, but this view is tenable only because some of the industrial problems would necessarily find their own solution as those affecting agriculture were successfuly attacked. The four basic problems of industry are materials, machinery, labor and markets. Materials and machinery require no special attention, as far as the industry of the Southeast is concerned. A rise in the purchasing power of the Southeastern farmer would automatically expand the market. Certain phases of the labor problem, too, would be alleviated, if not solved, by the reconstruction of agriculture.

Social planning for industry might concern itself to some extent with the development of extra-regional and foreign markets, labor organization and supply, and various technological questions of production and financing. Assuming, however, a measurable degree of success with the agricultural group, there will arise important questions concerning the integration of agriculture and industry. For one thing, a really prosperous agriculture would require a large number of new industries, both for processing its products and for supplying the goods it needs. It is inconceivable, for instance, that a well-balanced Southeastern agriculture could make shift with only three cheese factories in the entire region. Naturally, it would be one of the functions of a central planning authority to make available to managers and financiers adequate and accurate information regarding the industrial needs of specific subregions; and to act as intermediary between capital seeking investment and subregions requiring industrial development. Here, again, social planning is not so much under the necessity of introducing any new factors as of giving intelligent organization and direction to the energies already operating in the region.

In the same way the problems surrounding politics and government are of less immediate urgency than some others because, in the first place, some of them will be solved by the solution of the others and because, in the second place, the solution of the others will inevitably create new and not certainly predictable conditions which may require methods not guessed at as yet.

What plans, for example, should be made regarding the political status of the Negro? The only adequate answer to that question at present is another question, to wit, What Negro? The theorizing of the *Social Contract* and the language of the Declaration of Independence regarding "unalienable" rights are all very well, but every man who has had any experience of the hard realities of government knows that political capacity is profoundly affected by economic status. A political status appropriate to the nethermost element of the nethermost stratum of the nethermost agrarian economy in the country may not be—indeed, almost certainly will not be—appropriate to a prosperous, literate and increasingly adequate social group forming part of a wealthy and highly civilized society.

About all that can be predicted with certainty is that any political and governmental plan now designed to apply to specific situations would promptly become obsolete and perhaps pernicious as the situation changes. What is desirable, and all that is desirable, at once with regard to politics and government in the Southeast is an increased sense of reality, a readiness to face the facts as they are. The interdependence of the States is such a fact, and where it comes into collision with the theory of States' Rights, the theory must give way to the fact. The inadequacy of rugged individualism in a complex society is another fact, and no amount of political oratory about the sturdiness of American manhood can obliterate it. A tendency to rely on catch phrases, rather than reason, is a human failing from which the Southeast is no more exempt than any other region; but it happens at this juncture to be especially dangerous to the Southeast, and should therefore be guarded against with especial care.

All this, obviously, is no answer to the question of how to check the colossal waste that is swiftly depleting the moral and material resources of the Southeast. It is not intended to be an answer. He who would answer that question in detail would speak with the tongue of all philosophy. Odum certainly makes no pretense to such superhuman wisdom and is content merely to indicate the direction in which he thinks the answer lies.

To follow the direction he has indicated necessitates riding right over the immemorial obstacle of human fallibility. Count over the impediments to the adoption of regional planning for the Southeast and it is evident that each and every one lies somewhere in the great, desolate field of human frailty. What are the things that lie between the region and the attainment of a tremendously high level of civilization? Lack of sunshine, rainfall, fertility? On the contrary, in all these it is blessed far beyond nine-tenths of the earth. Lack of stone, timber, coal, oil, metals? On the contrary, it has them all in extraordinary abundance. Lack of man power? It has twenty-five million people and they are by far the most prolific in the country.

It lacks capital, and why? Because in the past it has been spendthrift beyond all imagining. For the small immediate profit, it has squandered the future fortune. For the little immediate ease, it has let the richness of its soil wash away; for the little immediate ease it has ensured future hard, grinding toil.

It lacks technical skill, and why? Because it has been as spendthrift of the minds of its sons as it has of its material wealth. It has permitted the mental horizons of its children to be circumscribed within narrow limits. Content with its own ways, it has never applauded and encouraged the intellectual curiosity that stimulates the young to look out into the great world, observe the manners and customs of other men, and enrich their own culture by the injection of alien ideas.

It lacks leaders, and why? Because it has always adored

the man of action and neglected, if not despised, the scholar. To this day it persists in sending to Washington men who as a class—and admitting a handful of conspicuous exceptions—are characterized first of all by an astounding ignorance of the manners and customs of men of other regions and other nations.

Regional planning, however, by its very definition implies forethought, prudence, the long view and a high respect for intellectual power. Capital, technical skill and the intellectual leadership that can be supplied only by highly-trained specialists are the deficiencies of the Southeast. It is for lack of these that the wastes have developed, and only by supplying these can the wastes be checked. They can be supplied, but only by a considerable shifting of Southern points of view and the development of new habits of thinking in the region.

Superficially, this may seem to be an assertion that Southern deficiencies can be supplied only by changing human nature, which is generally regarded as an impossible task. Perhaps, though, this task is not as impossible as it seems to be. At any rate, it has been accomplished once, with this very population; and what has been done once may be done again. Consider together two indubitable facts about the South. One is that its white population, which is politically, economically and culturally dominant, was drawn originally from the British Isles, in overwhelming proportion—that is to say, it was drawn from the same source as the population of the rest of the thirteen colonies. The other fact is that the population of the

Southeast is differentiated on a majority of seven hundred points from the population of any other region. That is to say, this population, once identical with the population of the Northeast and the British Isles, is now distinctly different from either. There is a change in human nature for you. It was a slow change, accomplished through three centuries; but it was a change, and there is no logical ground for declaring that a swifter change is impossible.

Moreover, if the question of racial capacity enters, the thing to remember is that this same stock has exhibited for many centuries an extraordinary power of survival. The peoples by whom the Southeastern States were populated have contrived to endure both the climatic ferocities of India and those of Maine; they flourish in their own rain-drenched islands and in the arid wastes of Australia. They have exhibited a well-nigh limitless power of adaptation; whatever was necessary to ensure their own survival in any environment they have managed to do, usually without appreciable loss of social adequacy and but rarely with any great loss of energy.

There is no reason to doubt that this power of survival is still in possession of the people of the Southeast. What is necessary, therefore, is not to endow them with the power of adaptation, but to persuade them to use it by pointing out the alternative to which the existing polity of the region is leading.

This is not hard to see. With more than thirty million acres of land gone and twice as much going by erosion, with twenty million tons of the remaining plant-food in the soil washing away annually, the ruin of the Southeast as an agricultural region is plainly in sight. Calculations no more abstruse than those of simple arithmetic will prove that fifty years more of waste at the present rate will do the work which, once done, cannot be undone save by the effort of centuries, if at all.

The complete wreck of the cotton economy is as plainly in sight. Dismiss from consideration, if you choose, the mechanical picker which, after all, is not yet on the market. Assume, if you will, that the very small adjustments which seem to be all that are necessary to its perfection will never be made. Still the end of cotton as the main economic reliance of the Southeast cannot be deferred for many years. The cost of production of cotton is steadily being reduced in other regions, whereas, when it changes at all, it tends to rise in the Southeast. The market is being steadily narrowed both by the introduction of substitutes for cotton fabrics and by the preëmption of foreign markets by foreign producers. Years, not decades, measure the time before the Southwest will be in position to raise enough cotton to supply such markets as are left. It is assuming no great risk to prophesy that the end of another ten years will see cotton farming in the Southeast so precarious and unprofitable that only victims of dire necessity will undertake it. Indeed, over large areas that is the situation now.

Then with its agricultural economy plainly crumbling, and with its agricultural lands swiftly being ruined, will the Southeast have the faintest hope of checking the human loss by emigration? Certainly not. The continuous narrowing of the field of opportunity will act as a powerful stimulant to emigration. Worse than that, it will mean a constantly rising percentage of wasted lives among the population remaining in the region.

In the words of a statesman who remains one of the region's great political heroes, it is a condition we are facing, not a theory. The Southeast has small patience with and small understanding of economic and social theorizing, but it understands perfectly the old dictum, Root, hog, or die.

Maybe it cannot overcome its interstate jealousies, its institutional jealousies, its sectarian jealousies. Maybe it can never reject peanut politics in favor of statecraft. Maybe it is incapable of smothering, at least for a time, its suspicion and distrust of theorists, of specialists, of men who have devoted their lives to the study of "ologies" and "isms."

Very well, then its goose is cooked. The situation is strange in that there appears to be no middle ground for the Southeast between a very high civilization and something indistinguishable from semibarbarism. There is no personal devil involved in this situation. There is no damnyankee, "full of envy, of rage, of hate, of gall," sitting in his noisome den and contriving the ruin of the South. Wall Street and the International Banker are not racking their brains to effect her destruction, despite the bellowing of countless campaign orators. Even if the Communists do claim that they kept nine Negroes unhanged at

Scottsboro, Alabama, there is not the slightest evidence that the Third International is paying much attention to the Southeast, and certainly the Soviets had nothing to do with bringing on her present difficulties. Not even the Capitalist System, that universal target for every marksman, can be blamed, except by indirection, for the washing away of arable land and the running away of the sprightliest and ablest Southern boys.

Waste is the enemy. Waste of land, waste of people, waste of time, waste of energy—these, and no outside foe, are throttling her. Therefore loud defiances and bitter complaints are simply more waste. There is one remedy, and one only—to stop the waste. But who is to accomplish that? The damnyankee cannot do it. All the bankers of Wall Street, either alone or miraculously allied with all the Communists in Moscow, cannot do it. Neither the Capitalist System, nor the Socialist System, nor any other system ever devised or dreamed of can do it. Nothing can do it but the intelligence and energy of the people of the region. It must be the people, too. Leaders are necessary, to be sure, and the abler they are, the better; but quite mediocre men, were they backed by a widespread and vigorous public opinion, could accomplish wonders toward halting many of the wastes that deplete the land.

Odum's estimate of twelve years may be too short a time for the rectification even of the worst mistakes the Southeast has made, but it is based on a great many careful calculations. Yet assuming that it is not half long enough, even twenty-five years would be no great matter for the transformation of a nation.

That it would be a transformation indeed is borne out by every statistical analysis that ingenuity can contrive. Let it be repeated for emphasis, there is no middle way. In one direction lies the horror portrayed in *Tobacco Road*. In the other lies the possibility of an agriculture developed as far beyond the best areas of the Middle States as they are beyond the average poor farm in the cotton belt; and with it an industry not gathered in huge concentrations, such as that around Pittsburgh, or Newark, but scattered widely and varied enough to serve the varied needs of the region. This, remember, is not guesswork; every necessary element, save organization, is already present in abundance. The purchasing and consuming power of the population would be raised to a level far beyond any that it has ever attained, which would mean an unprecedented stabilization of prosperity. In such a region opportunity would be so abundant that the problem of shifting population would be entirely one of selective immigration, not of checking emigration. In other words, here would be the basis of a magnificent civilization, and where the basis has been supplied, the superstructure has never failed to rise.

It can be done, but it cannot be done without taking thought. It cannot be done by building up one State at a time, regardless of the rest of the region. It cannot be done by building up one industry, or one farming region, or one race while paying no attention at all to the rest.

"Lord, bless me and my wife and my son, John, and his wife, us four and no more!" is a prayer that never was answered yet. The Southeast is a unit, the Southeast is an entity, and the eleven divisions into which the political geographers have laid it off do not, and cannot split its interests. It is a wasted land at present, and as such it is the poorest of all the regions; but it has that which, were it a well-tended land, would make it the Eden of America.

"I went by the field of the slothful, and by the vineyard of the man void of understanding;

"And, lo, it was all grown over with thorns, and nettles had covered the face thereof, and the stone wall thereof was broken down.

"Then I saw, and considered it well: I looked upon it, and received instruction.

"Yet a little sleep, a little slumber, a little folding of the hands to sleep:

"So shall thy poverty come as one that travelleth; and thy want as an armed man."